AMERICAS #1 SOURCE OF MONEY-MAKING IDEAS

Income
OPPORTUNITIES

HOME
BUSINESS
HANDBOOK

AMERICA'S #1 SOURCE OF MONEY-MAKING IDEAS

Income
OPPORTUNITIES

HOME BUSINESS HANDBOOK

EXPERT ADVICE FOR RUNNING A SUCCESSFUL BUSINESS OUT OF YOUR HOME

Including 100 Low-Investment Ideas

by the Editors of

INCOME OPPORTUNITIES® magazine

A PERIGEE BOOK

Perigee Books
are published by
The Putnam Publishing Group
200 Madison Avenue
New York, NY 10016

Library of Congress Cataloging-in-Publication Data

Income opportunities' home business handbook : expert advice for
running a successful business out of your home : including 100
low-investment ideas / by the editors of Income opportunities® magazine.
p.   cm.
ISBN 0-399-51611-5
1. Home-based businesses.   I. Income opportunities.   II. Title:
Home business handbook.
HD2333.I53   1990   89-71021   CIP
658'.041—dc20

Printed in the United States of America

1   2   3   4   5   6   7   8   9   10

CONTENTS

ACKNOWLEDGMENTS

The editors of *Income Opportunities*® magazine wish to express their appreciation and gratitude to the following authors whose articles helped in the compilation of this book. The articles originally appeared in *Income Opportunities*® magazine:

Paul J. Feeley, Gene Carpenter, Betty Ann Olmstead, Jan Dean, Linda S. Bozza, James Amodeo, Mildred Jailer, Priscilla Y. Huff, Fred Gebhart, Bill Stephenson, Sandra Holland, and especially Georganne Fiumara on whose column, "Your Home Business," much of this book was based.

With special thanks to Stephen Wagner, editor.

THE HOME BUSINESS BOOM

When Ronatta Greene was fifty-one years old, she did something that changed her life. Being a middle-aged woman made it difficult to find a rewarding job, so she bought a home computer and taught herself how to use it. With that purchase, Greene started her own home-based roommate-finder business, and her once uncertain future brightened and her limited life-options became virtually unlimited.

Greene fits just one profile of the types of people who are starting home businesses all across the U.S. Others include mothers who need to contribute to the family income, but who don't want to leave small children to do it; retirees who seek additional income to supplement pensions and their Social Security checks; professionals who have experienced "burn-out" and decide to strike out as entrepreneurs. Many are couples, especially those whose children are grown, who simply want something challenging and fulfilling to do with their lives.

How many work-at-homers are out there? According to their 1988 Work-at-Home Survey, Link Resources found that there are approximately thirteen million. The Internal Revenue Service also reports this thirteen million figure, based on people filing a Schedule C form with their annual income-tax returns. The U.S. Department of Labor predicts that by the mid-1990s, eighteen million people will be working at home, and they further predict that half of the country's work force could be working at home in ten to fifteen years!

Those are startling statistics. Not all of those people will be running home-based businesses. Many will be "telecommuting" to regular jobs via their home computers instead of traveling to the office. But as the nation turns even more from a manufacturing economy to a service economy, a large percentage of those work-at-homers will be owners of their own businesses.

Perhaps you will be one of them.

Today's home businesses range from service to manufacturing businesses and include those that operate from computer terminals tucked into spare rooms to those that use the tried-and-proven methods of ages past.

According to Anthony E. Whyte, director and founder of the American Home Business Association, some of the most successful home businesses are: computer consulting, bed and breakfast inns, home meal delivery, day-care centers, mail order, financial advice, accounting-on-wheels, home remodeling/repair, tax consulting, and diet/weight control advice.

There are many other types of businesses one can operate at home, of course, from crafts to beekeeping to computer programming. Most are completely independent ventures; that is, the owner is the creator and marketer of the product or service. Others are dealerships or distributorships which rely on an affiliated company for their products or materials (Avon, for example). Still others are franchises that have a home base rather than a storefront, and can be operated out of car or van.

You'll find 100 home business ideas for your consideration in Chapter 19 of this book.

CHAPTER ONE

WHY START A HOME BUSINESS?

The best part about starting a home-based business is the freedom it gives the individual to try his or her wings and create new opportunities. It's the challenge of being one's own boss and being responsible for one's own hours, salary, and destiny. It's the chance to try new ideas and to be creative, and the opportunity to work alone or with family and friends in pleasant, familiar surroundings. Operating a home business is a way to earn a living without joining the crowd in pin-striped suits or being caught in the early-morning rush hour. It's working where you can control your schedule and environment. It's pursuing an adventure.

A business started at home has a greater chance of success than one initiated in a commercial space. According to Dun and Bradstreet, 55 percent of small-business ventures fail within five years, whereas only about 20 to 25 percent of home businesses fail during an equivalent time period.

The reason home businesses have a better survival rate is that they have a much lower overhead than those operated out of a commercial space. Besides not needing to rent or buy business space, the deduction allowed for the business use of a home reduces the amount of taxes levied against the homeowner. Also, working at home saves the time that would normally be spent going to and from work, and it saves money by reducing transportation, wardrobe, and the other expenses associated with the workplace, from lunches to donations for pregnant secretaries.

Starting a business at home allows you to begin slowly, at your own pace. Most new home businesses are operated on a part-time basis until the kinks are worked out and they start to bring in a profit; however, this is nearly impossible for a new business that is situated in a rented space.

Running a successful business at home doesn't just happen. It takes a lot of verve to start a business, and you must be determined and excited about its potential and willing to put in the energy and hours needed to make it work.

A home business is not a get-rich-quick scheme, but it is a good way to live and work.

ARE YOU THE TYPE?

Working at home can be a dream come true or a nightmare—it all depends on you. Knowledge will be your key to success. Self-knowledge. Business knowledge. The more you know about your inner-most feelings and the basics of running a business, the more likely you are to realize your goals.

Let your answers to the following questions help you discover if you are suited for home business ownership. Answer the questions honestly. Even if you think that your answers indicate that you are not ready to own your own home business, don't give up. The very best part about working at home, as we've stated, is that you can start slowly, learn from your mistakes, and grow at your own pace. A world of possibilities will open up for you, and you can make the positive changes that will help you achieve your potential.

1. Why Do You Want to Work at Home?

Your boss is getting on your nerves and you don't think you can last one more day at your job. You hate the two-hour commute each day. You're tired of not earning as much as you are worth. Even though all of these problems can be solved by working at home, they are all very bad reasons for starting a home business. Your motivation should have positive roots, not negative. Most entrepreneurs just can't help moving in independent directions. The ideas flow and there just doesn't seem to be a reason not to proceed. Lack of money or help is no detriment for this kind of person—he or she will always find a way to manage. If your home business aspirations won't subside until you use your inner resources and put your ideas into action, then go for it. If you are just trying to escape a bad situation, then stop and re-evaluate.

2. Do You Know How to Make Mistakes?

Making mistakes, even outright failure at what you are trying to accomplish, might not be as bad as you think. Until you are willing to face rejection from others or make decisions that turn out to be off-target, you will not even have a chance to succeed. Mistakes are part of the growth and learning process. If you gain necessary knowledge and vital experience from your mistakes, they will be transformed into positive and valuable events. Ask yourself: "What's the worst thing that will happen to me if I make a mistake?" The answer will probably give you the courage to proceed.

3. What Do You Do When You Don't Know What to Do?

Believe it or not, this is the most important question on this list. Most people who want to start a home business don't know where to start. They expect others to give them ideas and then spoon-feed them the information they need to create a business. In this age of abundant information sources, learning what to do next can be as simple as reading a book—like this one. You can find all the answers you need, but you have to be willing to put forth the effort necessary to do your research.

Don't expect others who have spent many hours gathering information to just hand over the information to you just because you ask them. You can, however, observe or read about others who are already operating businesses which interest you and then imitate their methods of operation, their procedures for accessing the information they need, and their general attitudes. It may even be possible to enter into a networking relationship with some of your role models, but effective and long-lasting business relationships of this kind will endure only if you offer something in return. Even if you are just starting out, you might have more to offer than you imagine.

4. What Do You Do When No One Is Watching You?

Are you self-disciplined? When you are working at home, alone, you will either be your best friend or your worst enemy. As a business owner, if the work does not get done, only you and your business will suffer. You need to be self-motivated and really love the work you have chosen in order to lead a productive work life. It is necessary to get the work done before you take some time off. As the "boss," you can reward yourself for a job well done, but you are kidding yourself if you think that home business ownership will be your ticket to do anything you want, anytime you want.

5. Who Do You Trust?

Most home business owners start out handling all of the jobs that have to be done all by themselves. Some never even envision the day that they will not be able to adequately handle all of the work without help. But if your business is going to have the opportunity to grow, you will have to begin to relinquish your total control and delegate some work to others. The time will come when you need to trust a lawyer, an accountant, even some employees, to do jobs you formerly did yourself. When you start a home business, you first have to learn to trust yourself, then accept the help of others.

6. Are You a Gambler?

If you think that the right answer to this question is yes, you are wrong. Risk-taking is essential when starting a business, but every risk should be based on research and careful planning. Haphazard decisions made in haste will usually invite disaster. A risk-taker walks a tightrope with a safety net. The gambler will run across the wire without taking precautions—and may not survive the fall.

7. Are You a Daydreamer?

If you don't have a dream, you will never have a dream come true. Daydreams are the first steps to goal planning. Some call daydreaming "visualization." When you visualize yourself doing and accomplishing the steps necessary to meet your goals, you send messages to your subconscious which help you step beyond hoping and wishing and hard work to put your daydreams into actions.

8. Are You Versatile?

As a home business owner, you will wear many hats. In the beginning, it is necessary to know at least a little about every aspect of your business. Not only do you have to be skillful, you have to be willing to follow through on your responsibilities. If you are an artist, you cannot ignore the marketing end of your business. Keeping accurate records is essential, even if numbers are not your best friends. Every detail must be handled, and it is your responsibility to do it yourself, or make sure that someone else will.

9. Are You Persistent?

Most people do not fail, they give up. Persistence is probably the single most important attribute a new home business owner can possess. If you keep trying, you will eventually discover the right pathway. Calvin Coolidge realized this when he said, "Press on! Nothing in the world can take the place of persistence. Talent will not; nothing is more common than unsuccessful men with talent. Genius will not; unrewarded genius is almost a proverb. Education will not; the world is full of educated derelicts. Persistence and determination alone are omnipotent. The slogan 'Press On!' has solved and always will solve the problems of the human race."

And, we add, of the home business owner.

CHAPTER TWO

ADVANTAGES AND DISADVANTAGES OF A HOME-BASED BUSINESS

The sharp increase in the number of home-based businesses and other work-at-home situations in recent years indicates that they have distinct advantages over out-of-home jobs and businesses. Reduction of stress and gains in productivity are two primary advantages. Productivity gains of 40 to 50 percent were reported as realistic in a study of telecommuters conducted by the New York consulting firm of Electronic Services Unlimited.

Both stress reduction and productivity gains are due largely to the increased control you have over your work schedule and the type of breaks a home allows, such as walking around the block, stopping for a chat with the kids, or relaxing with a hot cup of homemade soup. A home office also eliminates common office stress factors such as fluorescent lights, ringing telephones, clattering equipment, buzzing conversation, and rush-hour traffic.

Parents who work at home report being closer to and more involved with their children, even if the children are very young and require some child care (inside or outside the home).

Home-office advantages can be broken down into three main categories: convenience, economy, and control. Let's examine each more closely.

CONVENIENCE

What could be more convenient than rolling out of bed at 9 A.M., grabbing a cup of coffee, and sitting down in the den to begin the day's work? Note that not even getting dressed was part of that scenario. Answering the previous day's business correspondence could be accomplished just as well in bathrobe and slippers as it could fully dressed. Only a home business allows this type of personal convenience.

There's no racing to catch the bus or commuter train, no battles with the rush-hour traffic. And although it is recommended that you establish a disciplined regimen for any home-based business, you can get up when you please, start work when you please, and quit for the day at your discretion. A home business is highly flexible. This is especially convenient when personal emergencies arise that require your immediate attention.

Mothers of young children especially can appreciate the convenience of a home-based career. They can earn extra money for the household and not sacrifice the importance and joy of caring for and raising their children. Time can be scheduled to send the kids off to school and greet them when they come home, to fix lunches, bandage scraped knees, and give out hugs. The modern woman who desires a career truly has the best of both worlds with a home business.

ECONOMY

To save on start-up costs is a primary reason many businesses are begun in the home. Office space, especially in the large cities, is quite expensive and simply not practical for many small businesses. Although many businesses of the type we discuss in this book are ideally suited for a home base, some could operate just as well in traditional office space. Indeed, as the business grows it may eventually be necessary to move out of the home to a downtown office. Until that level of success is achieved, however, the home office offers low overhead.

When you take office space, you're paying rent and furnishing it with desks, cabinets, carpeting, typewriter, and other supplies—most of which you probably already have at home. At home, you are already paying for the heat, air conditioning, and lights. You already have carpeting in the den. Why purchase them a second time? All of these things could easily add up to thousands of dollars. When you're beginning, you don't need these additional start-up costs if you can avoid them. Finding early success often requires that you run a "mean and lean" operation, cutting costs every possible way.

You don't have to dress for the office when you work at home, which means you'll save hundreds of dollars in clothing costs. Although you may still need business clothes for making occasional calls on clients, you won't need the extensive wardrobe that a formal office demands.

Many businesses that start in the home stay in the home for the reasons stated here. Yet even entrepreneurs who have larger ambitions for their venture find that a home-based operation is a good way to test the idea without putting capital at risk. If you are starting a mail-order business, for example, you don't really know how well your products will sell. It would be a mistake to rent office space and furnish it, and then learn that your products are flops. You have no profit, no income with which to pay your overhead. A more logical approach would be to start at home. The money you'll save will allow you to experiment with various products and various advertising appeals until you find a hit.

Another reason a home business is economically sound is tax savings. When you set aside an area of your home exclusively for your home business, the IRS allows you to deduct a percentage of your mortgage, electric bill, and other expenses from your tax return. See the end of Chapter 17 for more details on taxes and exactly what is deductible.

CONTROL

Most employees with traditional jobs work regular hours, day in and day out. Some of those people decide that they just can't hack it anymore. They're tired of the nine-to-five rat race, weary of the commuting, sick of the daily grind. Increasingly, as the years pass, a feeling of oppression grows, and they're haunted by the fear that they have lost control over their own lives. Many of these people start home-based businesses to regain that sense of control. Their hours may not be any shorter, but they are deciding the hours. They may have to live by strict rules of discipline, but they are rules of their own making. If they need a break, they take one without fear that the boss will be breathing down their necks; they are the boss. In a regular job they are paid the going rate; in their own home business, if they want a raise they work harder.

Having complete control over one's life, work, and destiny is essential for many people and their self-esteem.

DISADVANTAGES AND HOW TO DEAL WITH THEM

So far we've made running a home business sound rather appealing, but as with all things it has what some people would consider its bad points or downside. Even so, what we'll discuss here as disadvantages are often a matter of opinion or preference; what one person may consider a disadvantage another may think of as a distinct advantage.

One of the most difficult problems is the feeling of isolation. This can often be offset by joining professional business groups that meet once or more a month, by planning weekly lunches out with colleagues or other home workers, by networking with people both inside and outside your profession, and by telephoning several business people each day. These activities not only improve your mood, but can boost your business as well.

If you work for a company, you can cope with isolation by reserving one or two days a week to work at the company office, particularly if meeting with colleagues or clients is important. After one or two days a week crammed with meetings, you'll welcome the isolation of your home office. Of course, if you're someone who works best amidst a flurry of activity, and you thrive on the social stimulation of a daily lunch with colleagues and sharing office gossip, working at home may not be for you.

Friends dropping by, children running through your office, and the temptations of television or your favorite hobby can also play havoc with your home-office life. However, after a period of adjustment during which you lay out the rules regarding your office routine and maintain the self-discipline to adhere to them, these problems usually diminish.

In fact, you soon may find it difficult to get away from your work.

Susan Jones, a freelance writer whose "office" was a desk in the corner of her living room, loved working at home, but was often frustrated by the feeling that she could never leave her work.

"No matter what I was doing, I could see my desk and all the work I needed to do," Jones says. "It didn't matter that my computer was turned off and my office 'closed.' Just the sight of it made me feel like I should be working."

Jones resolved the problem by moving into a larger apartment and establishing an office in a spare bedroom. Once her desk was out of her line of vision, she could enjoy her leisure time.

Although working at home gives you the advantage of being near your children, it can be a disadvantage, especially with very young children. You may want to hire someone to care for your young child in your home on a part- or full-time basis, or you may opt to place your child in a child-care center during your busiest hours.

Hard work and long hours are often unavoidable for the home-based worker. Are these disadvantages? They can be if you're used to regular hours. But, as we've shown above, many people start their own businesses to get away from the nine-to-five routine.

So have no illusions, your home-based business—no matter what it is—will require discipline, dedication, your utmost energy, time, and enthusiasm if it is to succeed. It is not a way to get rich quick, and should not be considered an easy way out of a daily grind. What this all boils down to is that a home-based business is not for the lazy.

One other disadvantage of owning your own business is that you have to make sure you are insured. When you are working for someone else, most likely you are covered by a combination of various group insurance programs: disability, major medical, dental, Blue Cross/Blue Shield, and unemployment. If you're working for yourself and you are uninsured, a major health problem can wipe you out.

There are solutions to the problem of insurance, and they are covered later in this book.

CHAPTER THREE

PART-TIME OR FULL-TIME?
... AND SOME SUCCESS
STORIES OF BOTH TYPES

When considering a home-based business, many people wonder if they should start on a part-time basis or plunge right in full-time. Without a doubt, it is best to start slow. Don't quit your regular job just yet. What if you are currently unemployed? Believe it or not, it is recommended that you first find full-time work to support you and your family while setting up your home business part-time. It is going to take a while for your business to get off the ground and running at a rate that will pay the bills. Provide some security first by ensuring that you receive a regular paycheck, and in your spare time start planning and building your home business.

Beginning on a part-time basis has several other advantages:

• It allows you to experiment with various methods of operation, products, equipment, and advertising. Eventually you will hit on the right combination that will lure customers, satisfy your clients, and bring in the highest profits.
• It keeps your investment to a minimum.
• You may find that you never want to operate on a full-time basis, satisfied with the extra part-time income that your sideline business will generate.
• Starting small allows you to learn as much as you can about the

particular business, and to make inevitable mistakes without devastating consequences.

Are there advantages to starting off full-time? First of all, to even consider such a drastic change in routine and lifestyle, you'd have to be certain that you could handle it financially. If you have a lot of money to play around with, and providing for your family is not a worry, then you might want to give it a shot. The advantage here is that your full-time concentration and devoted energy to your home business might bring about greater success more quickly. Notice, even here we say "might" since there are no guarantees.

On the whole, we recommend starting part-time. Get to know the business, learn all the ins and outs, and experiment to optimize your operation and perfect your ad campaign. Take your time. Your growing profits will tell you when it's time to go full-time, if that's what you want. And who knows, it may be sooner than you imagine. Here are some full- and part-time home business success stories to give you an idea of what has worked for a variety of entrepreneurs in different walks of life.

ELLEN MEEHAN AND MARY WALKER: IN STITCHES

They are housewives and mothers of young children. Now they are also budding entrepreneurs. Meehan and Walker discovered a way to remain at home with their youngsters, continue in their roles as homemakers, while contributing to their family incomes and broadening their own horizons. "In Stitches" is a small, home-operated business featuring quality handcrafted items. Their line of crafts, which initially consisted of ribbon baskets, macrame plant hangers, and a variety of Christmas items, has now expanded to include fabric frames, quilted wall hangings, a variety of other decorative items, and a seasonal line for spring/summer and fall/winter.

In Stitches began with a $400 joint investment, funds each of the women took from their household "pin" money. Six months later, not only has their initial investment returned, but they are showing a profit. Initially, to launch the business and cover the cost of supplies, inventory, and advertising, Meehan and Walker had reinvested all of their profits back into the business. At the six-month mark, however, they began to enjoy the monetary results of their venture. The percentage of the profits farmed back into the business has been drastically reduced from 100 percent to 40 percent, or 20 percent for each partner. And the prospects for the future look brighter still.

What makes Meehan and Walker's success story so exciting is that neither of these women was formally trained in her skill; neither had ever had experience in establishing or operating a business; and neither relies on day-care services to provide for her children's needs. They are average homemakers, different only in that they had the courage to invest in a dream and work hard to make it become a reality.

Selecting their craft line was not a problem. Simplicity patterns and craft books were carefully scrutinized, and a wide variety of salable crafts resulted. There is an emphasis on *usable* decorative items such as quilted tissue boxes, macrame towel holders, and doorstoppers.

At the outset, both women agreed that selling at home parties was the most logical and viable route for them. To launch the business and exhibit their crafts, their first venture was an "open house" conducted at Meehan's home just prior to the winter holiday season. The open house had a dual purpose: to introduce the business and market its craft line, and to initiate the booking of home parties. It was successful in both respects. Not only was their entire stock sold out, but, perhaps more important, additional orders were taken and several buyers agreed to host a home party.

Despite their success, both women point out that their major commitment remains to their families, and their work schedule must be flexible to meet the demands of their very young children. But their business has taken on a personal importance. "It gives me something else to think about," says Walker. "I have to feel I can accomplish something other than housework. This is for my self-fulfillment, my own self-worth."

VINCE TAYLOR: TAYLORVISION

Vince Taylor is a self-made millionaire who started shooting video as a hobby in Clearwater, Florida. In 1981, Taylorvision started videotaping at a small profit using simple and inexpensive Radio Shack components. "I videotaped anything I could—weddings, dances, bar mitzvahs, you name it," says Taylor. In 1983, Taylor grossed $50,000 working out of his home. But he didn't stop there.

When Taylor began, he contacted local businesses and produced videos for realtors, restaurant owners, and any other business person who accepted his services. He went on to produce an original idea called the "Welcome Channel" and sold it to local hotels. "I ran cable to their rooms," he says, "and on an unused channel showed videos of things in the Clearwater area such as shops and activities. Of course, that also meant I could go to the local stores and produce low-rent commercials for them, to show on the Welcome Channel."

Taylor used direct mail to make contacts until a local NBC affiliate station hired him as its area "stringer." As time passed, Taylor moved on to higher-paying contracts. Taylorvision grossed over $3 million in 1989.

As Taylor's experience testifies, you don't need expensive equipment or professional experience at the beginning, just a little imagination, patience, and perseverance.

JERRIE MARKIEWICZ: TISKET-A-TASKET GIFT BASKETS

Jerrie Markiewicz had tried to earn extra money by selling craft items at craft fairs, but met with little success. Discouraged, she sold or gave away all her craft items. However, she did not want to resort to a "regular" job because she had a small child to care for. At about this time, a brother of one of Markiewicz's friends, a deli owner, asked if she would make some gift baskets for a few of his customers as Easter gifts. His customers loved her baskets, which gave Markiewicz the idea for a home business.

Markiewicz borrowed $5,000 from her joint bank account for start-up costs. She reports, "I'm proud to say I paid it back within a year. But I believe a person needs at least that amount to start this business."

Markiewicz was sure that creating gift baskets was a business she could succeed with. She made some sample baskets, purchasing the items at a discount department store. She liked the results, and so did her husband, who encouraged her to pursue the venture.

Markiewicz attended seminars offered by the U.S. Small Business Administration held at Lehigh University in Bethlehem, Pennsylvania. Here she learned the procedures needed to establish a small business. Then she registered a fictitious name for the business—Tisket-a-Tasket Gift Baskets—and obtained a packet from her state which contained instructions for keeping sales tax records and other business tips. Markiewicz also got a business-tax number and then checked with her borough officials about regulations. They told her she could not have a retail store in her house or use more than twenty-five square feet of the downstairs for her business. All of these regulations fitted into Markiewicz's business plan.

To begin advertising her business, Markiewicz had attractive business cards printed, along with a beautiful brochure which she illustrated herself. The brochure describes the baskets in detail with the prices and other services Markiewicz offers. Then she visited nearby business offices and distributed decorative glass jars filled with imported candies. Along with this complimentary gift she attached her business card and left several brochures.

How did Markiewicz determine her prices? In a magazine article she read about a woman with a similar business, it said that the woman doubled whatever her materials cost her. "If it costs her twenty dollars to create a basket," says Markiewicz, "she'll charge forty dollars. But in the area that I live, I believe if I would double my costs, my baskets would cost too much to sell. I charge about thirty percent above what it costs me to make a basket. I might eventually have to charge more, though, because my accountant says I don't charge enough!"

Markiewicz offers other services with her baskets. She delivers "free" within ten miles. She also accepts Visa and MasterCard. To be eligible to accept credit cards, she went to a full-service bank. "They helped me set up a business account," she says, "and instructed me to keep it for three months, and then I could apply to accept the credit cards."

What does Markiewicz hope for the future of her business? "I hope to get my product more exposure," she says. "I still need to learn better marketing techniques." But Markiewicz has plans to attend seminars on this subject sponsored by the Small Business Administration. With that kind of determination and persistence, she leaves little doubt that her Tisket-a-Tasket Gift Baskets will be a great success.

ELIZABETH ROSE DICKERSON: GARDEN CONSULTING

When Elizabeth Rose Dickerson of Quakertown, Pennsylvania, gave birth to her second child, she knew she would not be able to afford child care for two. Elizabeth is a trained horticulturist who worked for the Burpee Seed Company of Warminster, Pennsylvania. Her main job was to answer customers' questions about gardening. "I really enjoyed the challenge of the customers' varied questions," explains Dickerson, "so I decided to advertise myself as a gardening consultant and to set up my own home business."

What she thought would be a part-time venture has turned into a full-time business. She charges customers a one-time $50 consulting fee and $25 to $30 an hour teaching courses to various community groups. "I'm busier than when I worked for Burpee, and my business has gone in so many different directions that I'm never bored," says Dickerson.

When Dickerson began her business as a garden consultant, she distributed business cards and signs in local garden shops and stores announcing her services as a "horticulturist/consultant." Homeowners began to call her with various questions about their gardening needs.

If anyone so desires, Dickerson will design annual and perennial gardens plus special "theme" gardens: butterfly, colonial, fragrance, tea, moonlight, or whatever combination the homeowner decides on. In addition she will test the soil, advise how to improve it, and give general gardening advice.

Dickerson also teaches nursing-home residents on a regular basis. She gives these sessions several times a week and charges $25 an hour. Dickerson says, "It is the most rewarding experience I have ever had."

Dickerson believes this type of business is in demand, especially in communities where avid gardeners live. "The initial investment is only about $200 (business cards, posters, basic tools). "The work can be both physically and mentally challenging, but the potential rewards are there. If you persist, you can earn up to $75 an hour (during the busiest seasons). However, the intangible rewards can be even greater as you see your students become as enthusiastic about gardening as you are!"

JOHN GIACCHI: JOHN'S AQUARIUM MAINTENANCE

"They say I'm into a New Age enterprise," says John Giacchi. "But to me, it's something I love doing. It's almost like a hobby. And it makes a profit."

Mr. Giacchi runs John's Aquarium Maintenance, based in Hillsdale, New Jersey. His business proves that a part-time home-based business doesn't necessarily have to operate in one's home. Giacchi makes calls on his clients, but his base of operations is in his home; it is where he does his accounting and paperwork.

During any given month, he visits approximately 100 fish-tank locations in doctors' waiting rooms, building lobbies, offices, restaurants, cocktail lounges, private residences, and, most frequently, dentists who feel a fish tank in the waiting room can relax uptight patients. "It's my responsibility to make the fish tank look as good as possible and to keep the fish healthy," says John.

John's job includes changing the water, cleaning the tank and filter, replacing charcoal, and eliminating algae. He also repairs or replaces tank motors, pumps, and heater elements, and checks on the well-being of the fish.

John travels from client to client in a large service vehicle resembling a van that he bought used for $7,000 plus a $150 charge for painting the name of his service on both sides. The vehicle is kept stocked with approximately $500 worth of cleaning equipment and supplies; among them, hoses, siphons, buckets, and spare parts for tank accessories. John also pays $1,500 a year for general liability insurance geared to a small service business, workman's compensation, and vehicle insurance, which is a legal requirement in New Jersey. His major expense is driving back and forth to his many clients. John estimates that he spends approximately $300 per month on gasoline.

John's part-time business earns him as much as $25,000 a year. His charges for the monthly aquarium-maintenance visits range from as little as $40 to as much as $150 for an oversized tank located at a site that requires lengthy travel time. John also feeds fish on a regular basis for vacationing clients; there is a special charge for this service. And he has noticed that "the owners don't mind paying from seven to fifteen dollars a visit because they know the fish are in good hands."

CHAPTER FOUR

FINDING ROOM IN YOUR HOME AND SETTING UP YOUR HOME OFFICE

With a spare bedroom, den, or other room, and a budget of about $3,000, you can outfit a small office with a computer, printer, copying machine, and telephone answering machine.

A larger office with room for one or two employees and a reception area for clients—if your business requires such an area—takes only a little more space and a few more dollars. And, conversely, if you don't need all the fancy hardware, a home office with a good typewriter and some filing space will cost substantially less.

When real-estate appraisers Jaylene and Homer Hahn moved their office into their home, they converted a large back room that enclosed their swimming pool. They drained the pool, covered it with a platform, laid carpet, and built a partition to divide the area into a reception area and a private office. The cost of the conversion was less than $5,000.

"This is the only way for us. We'll never move out into another office," Jaylene says. "We're near the kids, more productive, and don't have all the stress we had when we worked outside our home."

DEFINE THE SPACE

You must first clearly define your work space depending upon the amount of privacy you need, as well as the rules regarding working hours, interruptions, etc. A home office—a real office—can help you create the appropriate atmosphere in which to conduct business. And keeping your business materials all in one place will help you to protect the continuity of your work.

If you do not have a spare bedroom or den, you will have to use your imagination to find your office space. You can consider converting your garage, basement, laundry room, walk-in closet, an alcove, or breakfast nook. If all else fails, a corner of your bedroom or living room can be converted into an office by using room dividers such as free-standing shelves, office partitions, or even just a curtain.

When making your choice of location, there are some factors to consider. You will want to choose a place which is out of the mainstream of your household. Select a place that makes you feel good, one which you will look forward to working in. If the only space available is a dingy basement or other undesirable spot, do all you can to make it a pleasant oasis. Some paint, a few plants, and good lighting can transform any drab corner. Set up your office so that it will reflect your business and your personal style. If people will be coming to your office, try to choose a location that is close to an entrance.

Choose decorations and furnishings that you can afford, knowing that you can upgrade equipment as your business grows. Don't despair if you cannot buy more than a desk, chair, and telephone right now. Henry David Thoreau once said, "I would rather sit on a pumpkin and have it all to myself than be on a crowded velvet cushion." Your office is yours, and having this space to call your own is tangible proof that you are an independent business person. You will gain respect, self-confidence, and the opportunity to work more efficiently when you separate the place where you work from the rest of your home.

If you don't want clients coming to your office, work out a system that establishes specific locations where you will conduct meetings and the delivery and pickup of important papers. Good options for meetings are clients' offices or a quiet restaurant.

FURNITURE AND SUPPLIES

Shop carefully for office furniture. The wrong desk height and an uncomfortable chair can cause back pain, fatigue, and reduced productivity. If you need it, buy furniture that is practical and comfortable. Lighting, too, plays an important role in productivity. Your home office should be well lit without glaring lights. Use soft-light light bulbs and avoid fluorescent lighting; studies have shown that they can increase stress, and there are links with other health problems.

List the furniture and supplies you need. Buy supplies in bulk. Not only will you save money, but you'll save shopping time, and you won't run out of supplies at critical moments.

When shopping for a computer, copier, and other office equipment, check the options of renting or leasing versus buying. Never buy without first checking such points as ease of use, range of capabilities, noise of operation, and ease of equipment repairs and servicing.

Only you will know what specific equipment you'll need to operate your particular business, and we won't go into that here. In other words, if you'll be starting a home/apartment cleaning service, we're not going to tell you in this section that you'll need a couple of mops, soap, and dust rags. We refer only to the office part of your business—what you'll need to conduct business from day to day. Of course, because home-based businesses are so varied we can only generalize about supplies and equipment, but here is a list of what you will need, what you might need, and you probably won't need.

WHAT YOU WILL NEED

Desk and chair. Obviously, you'll need a place to work and sit. A small desk with a few drawers, space perhaps for a typewriter (see below), and some elbow room is adequate. You might be able to pick up a nice used desk at a garage sale, but if you want a new one, it'll cost upwards of $130; the chair, about $70.

Typewriter. No home office should be without a good typewriter. Don't think you can get along with handwritten letters on note paper— no one will take your business seriously. If you don't already have one, you can pick up a good electric typewriter (you may actually find it difficult to find a new manual typewriter these days) with correction memory for about $140. Models with built-in dictionaries and spelling correctors run about $200. There are many models in between, of course, that have such features as automatic indentation, centering, and justification. Choose the one that suits your needs and budget.

Business telephone. Install a separate telephone line for your home business. Unless you have a small mail-order business in which you will rarely if ever have contact with customers and suppliers, there are many reasons to have a separate line, but the most important is this: when the telephone rings, you will know it is a business call. This simple bit of information has many implications. When you answer your business line, you will always use your name or the given name of your business; this will give you instant credibility. You will have control over who answers your phone and what is said to the caller. For times when you do not want to take business calls, or when you are not available, you can use an answering service or a good-quality answering machine (see below).

Your own business line will help you further separate your business from your personal life. When you are in the office working, you will be free to answer your own telephone and know that your business calls will not be held up.

When your business has its own telephone, you will be entitled to a listing in the Yellow Pages, and a larger advertisement if you want to pay the additional cost. Your telephone number will be listed under your business name in the phone company's directory assistance so that new customers will be able to locate you by name. These are excellent ways to obtain new clients. And when they call, you can feel sure that your telephone will be answered in an easy-to-understand, professional manner.

Answering machine. At a cost of about $100, an answering machine can insulate your business from inevitable household disturbances. If the baby is screaming or the dog is barking at the mailman, you can turn on your answering machine, and your telephone will be answered in a calm, professional manner. When you break for lunch or at the end of a work day, your answering machine will take your business calls so that your personal time will not be interrupted. The client who knows you work at home and wants to chat at midnight will just have to call back in the morning.

Be careful to choose a reliable answering machine that has all of the features you will need. Make sure that it will be easy to retrieve your messages from another telephone when you are not at home (many provide a "beeper" device for this purpose), that there is a fast-forward button so you will not have to listen to old messages to get to the new ones, and that the machine is voice activated so that the caller who has a long message will not be cut off. Record a short, clear, outgoing message. Music or funny messages do not belong on a business line.

Stationery. Your business cards, stationery (letterhead and envelopes), and brochures—all of your printed materials—represent you and your business, so they should be carefully designed and printed. You may not need the highest-quality paper available, but a good-quality paper that feels good to the touch, combined with an appealing typeface and an exclusive logo will give the recipient an unspoken message. The first impression that your mailing makes will determine whether or not it is read.

Business cards are important for any business. Have a couple hundred printed at first. It should feature the name of your company, your name, street address or mailing address, and phone number. You may also want to include some actual information about your business or a slogan:

ADAM'S LAWN CARE

"We take care of your lawn
as if it were our very own."

- Seeding
- Watering
- Trimming
- Fertilizing
- Landscaping
- Sprinklers installed

105 E. Lansing St., Hyville, NY 11634   (516) 555-2234

You may even want to invest in the new photo business cards which feature a photograph of either you or some pertinent aspect of your business. They are very appealing, and customers are quite reluctant to throw them away because they are so unusual. Which brings us to the real importance of business cards: they are mini advertisements for your business. To whomever you give them, or wherever you leave one, you leave behind a little, but powerful, reminder of what you have to offer.

Have several hundred each of letterhead and envelopes printed in matching type and color. The more you have printed, the less the printing costs per piece, but don't go overboard and print a thousand or more. You don't want so much stationery that it takes up too much of your precious home-office space. Besides, if you move or change your phone number, you'll have to discard all that useless paper.

Shop around for a printer. You'll be surprised at the differences in prices you'll find among printers. Choose a printer who offers a good price and who will help you choose the right paper stock, typeface, color, and design.

File Cabinet. Keeping records is a necessity for any business, and so a file cabinet will be needed. A two-drawer metal file cabinet sells for about $45. Don't forget you'll need file hangers and folders in which to keep the papers.

Calculator. Chances are you probably already have a hand calculator lying around the house. If not, you'll need one on your home-office desk, whether to add orders or figure your taxes. A simple hand-held solar calculator (it needs no batteries) can be purchased for about $12. For business purposes, however, you may need a calculator that also prints on paper. These go for about $40 and up.

Shelving. You can make your own shelves or buy ready-made shelves at any home-improvement store. Most likely you'll need shelf space for reference books, a small amount of inventory, and miscellaneous items.

Miscellaneous. Desk items you'll need include stapler and staples, a box of blue pens, a box of red pens, a box of pencils, pencil sharpener, erasers, typing paper, paper clips, rubber bands, cellophane tape, Wite-Out, and Rolodex or file cards.

Special. It's impossible for us to know all of the things you will need for your business, but some special items that might very well be needed are: mailing labels, imprinted invoices and statements, cartons, packing tape, large envelopes, various rubber stamps, and ledger paper.

To keep your expenses to a minimum, don't buy any of the above unless you really need it. Certainly you should not under any circumstances go out and buy everything we have listed above before you start your new business. Buy *what* you need *when* you need it, and always shop around for the lowest prices.

WHAT YOU MIGHT NEED

Included under this heading is equipment that would be useful, but should be purchased only if: (a) you know you'd really use it to help your business profit and grow; (b) you can afford it.

Word processor. If your business entails quite a bit of writing, it would be worthwhile to purchase a dedicated word processor. The capabilities of this kind of machine lie halfway between a modern electric typewriter and a full-blown personal computer (PC). They usually come equipped with monitors, internal memory capacity, the ability to save files on disks, built-in dictionaries, programmable page formats, variable fonts, and built-in printers. Prices run at about $600 and up. All these machines do, however, is word processing. If you want broader capabilities, you'll want a . . .

Personal computer. Besides word processing, PCs can be of assistance to the home business owner in a great number of ways. Be advised, however, that none of these capabilities are built into the PC; they require software programs for each task. A PC with a database program can keep track of your inventory, maintain a customer list, print out mailing labels (you'll also need a printer), do invoices, and much more. A spreadsheet program can handle many of your financial tasks, including cost projections, profit and loss statements, etc. A checkbook program can maintain a checkbook, write checks, and balance itself at the end of the month. In short, a PC can serve many functions for just about any business. And although many businesses do very well with a typewriter, card file system, and ledger book, many small-business people who trade up to PCs wonder how they got along without them.

Today you can buy a PC with two disk drives, monitor, and printer starting at about $1,500. For the best buys, check your newspaper for local sales or get a copy of *Computer Shopper* magazine.

As for software, your best bet might be to buy what is called an integrated software package which combines a word processor, database, and spreadsheet all in one. Check with your local dealer for details and assistance.

More detailed information about the role of the computer in the home office can be found in the following chapter.

WHAT YOU WON'T NEED

Under this heading is equipment that most home businesses will *not* need. Of course, there are some businesses providing certain services that couldn't do without them. These items can be convenient, but when weighed against the price you must pay for them, they can easily be dismissed. If their price drops (as sometimes they do), they become more attractive.

Copier. It's rare that you'll find a home business with its own copy machine. With price tags of $500 or more, it's easy to see why it's probably more practical to find other solutions to making copies of documents: using good ol' carbon paper; running off an extra copy on your printer; or using a copy machine at a local copy shop or library.

Fax machine. The prices of these neat little gadgets are still pretty hefty—starting at around $600. For the few times you'll absolutely, positively have to get it there overnight, it's better to use an overnight carrier service.

Anything fancy. Keep your office simple when you're starting out. It'll improve your bottom line and make your new business profitable that much quicker.

CHAPTER FIVE

THE ROLE OF THE COMPUTER

We have mentioned above how a computer, although not absolutely essential, can be very helpful to the home-based business on a number of levels. The decision of whether or not to buy a computer is strictly up to you, of course, based on the following question: Will its cost and the time it takes to learn to use it be justified by the speed and efficiency it will bring to your business?

For many small businesses, the answer is yes. Many home business operators have found that after reluctantly buying a personal computer, they put it to use and then wondered how they got along before without it.

These are the most common functions computers are performing for business:

Inventory Management. The computer keeps records of items in stock, tells you when to reorder, and provides reports of sales history and inventory cost.

Payroll. It prepares checks, stores information on deductions and takes them, keeps information about employee status and other relevant information.

Accounts receivable. It maintains credit and account status of each of your customers, and prepares invoices.

Accounts payable. Tracks current accounts payable, forecasts cash requirements, records information on purchase orders.

General ledger. Records financial transactions and generates balance sheets and income statements.

Word processing. Efficient editing of text and automatic typing of letters, envelopes, and any business documents.

Business analysis. Business data of any kind can be analyzed and forecasts made.

In a nutshell, the computer reduces the tedious paperwork involved with the daily business effort, performs such tasks better and faster, solves complex business problems, and often reduces operating costs. It also brings order to what is often chaos.

BUYING A COMPUTER

Many people, after they have decided that a computer might help in their home business, have ventured into the computer stores and have been frightened to death. They are frightened of what they don't know. Some computer stores don't help much. Their salespeople love to bowl their customers over with remarks like, "Yeah, this baby will balance the books for you. It's got one meg of RAM, one half-meg floppy drive, a forty-meg hardcard, and an 80286 running at twelve megahertz."

Huh?

You're not interested in how a computer works or how much memory it has. You want to know if it does the kind of jobs that will help you establish or operate your business more efficiently. When a computer salesperson asks how much memory you want in your system, don't say "640K" or "one megabyte." Just say something like, "Enough to track three thousand names or addresses" or "Enough to develop project-management charts for a two-person, home-based typing service." Not only does this make it easier on you, it places the responsibility of matching your needs with the right computer on the salesperson. This has some very important legal ramifications.

Does this mean you can forgo all of the computer's technicalities? Not really. You still should know some of the buzz words when you shop for a system. You should know what some of the words mean— like bit, byte, RAM, and ROM—so you can make a wise buying decision. We advise taking a trip to the library and checking out some books on computer basics.

THE BASIC HOME-OFFICE SYSTEM

If you decide you need or want a computer for your home-based business, you will need the computer itself (comes with keyboard), a monitor (TV screen), a disk drive, software, and a printer. Let's take a look at them one at a time.

The Computer. Essentially, there are four basic computer systems you can purchase for your home business: IBM (or clone or compatible); Apple; Amiga; Atari ST. There are other small computers available, but for business purposes these are the main four.

By far, IBMs and their clones and compatibles (Epson, Headstart, Leading Edge, Tandy, and many others) are the most widely used type of computer for business. These computers also have the widest variety of business software available (see below). A standard setup usually comes with one floppy drive and 640K of internal memory, quite adequate for anything you'll want to do. Generally, the clones are substantially less expensive than the IBM models.

In second place in popularity is the Apple Macintosh computer. This system doesn't have as much in the way of business software as the IBM, but does have a variety of programs available for the functions mentioned above. The Macintosh is usually favored as a computer for desktop publishing, and is more expensive than the IBM clones. The Apple II and Apple IIgs are different types of computers than the Macintosh; the Macintosh relies more on a mouse interface—that is, you use a mouse to make choices and enter data—than a keyboard. There are many business software titles available.

The Atari ST also relies heavily on its mouse interface, which many people find very easy to use for certain applications, such as graphics. The ST was, in fact, designed with color graphics in mind. Most business software, however, such as word processing and spreadsheets, needs keyboard input. The ST does have a keyboard, naturally, but there are not as many business software titles available, although the list is growing. The ST comes with $1/2$ megabyte of internal memory and has a reasonable price.

The Amiga line of computers from Commodore—the Amiga 500 and Amiga 2000—are perhaps the most advanced computers you can purchase for home use. The Amiga's strength lies in its color graphics capabilities and its ability to multitask—that is, to run more than one program at a time. Although there are not nearly as many business software titles available for the Amiga as there are for the IBM, there are enough titles to fulfill your business requirements. One further advantage that the Amiga has is the ability to emulate both an IBM and a Macintosh! With a Bridgeboard installed, the Amiga can run virtually any software designed for the IBM, opening all of those programs to the Amiga. And a recently introduced program called A-Max allows the Amiga to run all Macintosh software! These capabilities make the Amiga the most versatile computer available.

You'll have to pay for all of these capabilities, of course, and depending on what you will be using the computer for, it may be worth it to you. But if you just need a computer with which to do your word processing, handle your books, and manage your customer list, an IBM clone will be your best buy.

Monitor. With most computers, you must buy the monitor—the TV-like viewing screen—separately. Most business people opt for either a green or amber monochrome (one-color) monitor. If you plan on the extensive use of graphics, a color monitor will be more to your liking. There are many types of monitors available in a choice of resolutions. Check your dealer.

Disk Drive. Virtually all computers come equipped with at least one floppy disk drive. One disk drive is essential for both loading programs and storing data either on 5¼″ or 3½″ disks. Having two drives is better since they allow you to copy disks for backup purposes more rapidly. A better combination is one floppy drive and one hard drive. A hard drive, usually installed inside the computer, uses no removable disks but can store vast amounts of information which you can access at great speed. Again, ask your dealer which drive combination and which size hard drive would be most suitable for your particular business.

Software. Just as a VCR is worthless without videotapes to play on it, so is a computer worthless without software. As mentioned above, there is adequate business software available for all of the computer brands named above, but you should be aware that the programs can be expensive. So when you are pricing a computer system, figure in the cost of the software that you will need. The best buys for you will be integrated programs—programs that have many functions incorporated into one package. The most common combination is word processor, spreadsheet, and database; some packages include communications software and sundry other "desktop" utilities such as notepads, calculators, and time managers.

Printer. You will undoubtedly need a printer. Your word processor won't do you much good unless you can print out your work. There is a wide variety of printers from which to choose, the three basic types being dot matrix, letter quality, and laser printers. Dot matrix printers are fast, can produce near-letter-quality type, can usually produce characters in different sizes, and can print out graphics. Letter quality printers are slower but can produce high-quality type; most have removable printwheels for changing typefaces. Laser printers are the fastest of the lot, produce high quality, and are, naturally, the most expensive. A home business would probably be best off purchasing a high-quality (24-pin) dot matrix printer. It will give both the speed and letter quality you'll need.

Add to all of the above the sundry supplies you will need to keep the system running: appropriate cables, disks, printer ribbons, and computer paper.

Add up all these costs and again ask: Will the cost and the time it takes to learn to use the system be justified by the speed and efficiency it will bring to my business?

CHAPTER SIX

PREPARING YOURSELF AND YOUR FAMILY

The day you make the decision to go into business for yourself will probably be one of the most exciting days in your life. You'll feel like you own the world and you're certain that everything you touch will soon turn to gold. Everyone would like to quit his job tomorrow morning and open his own business the next day. All too often, over-eager entrepreneurs do just that. However, such an action can have devastating results. Before leaving the security of a regular paycheck, it is important to prepare yourself and your family.

Preparation of the entire family for opening day should involve the following steps:

1. Cut monthly personal cash requirements to a minimum and plan a tight budget.
2. Discuss the loss of a monthly or weekly paycheck and how each family member must help reduce costs.
3. Maximize cash on hand when leaving a job.
4. Make any arrangements for credit or loans before quitting a job.
5. Check your credit rating.
6. Secure adequate health insurance before leaving your present job.

7. Have a family discussion about how this new venture will affect each member of the family.
8. If the family is to be involved in operating the business, discuss what is expected of each person involved.

Now let's take a look at each step more closely.

THE FAMILY BUDGET

Since most first-time entrepreneurs have limitations on the amount of available cash, a strict personal budget is very important. It doesn't matter whether the husband or the wife is going to run the business. If that person has been working, a change will result in the monthly cash availability.

It is important to review all monthly payments for mortgages, cars, and credit cards, and make certain that all are current. Also check to see if there is any leeway for late payments, should that be necessary. If any of the payments can be eliminated, such as selling an extra car, do so. *The time prior to opening a business should be spent cutting personal monthly costs to the bare minimum.*

For most people, this will be their first time without a regular paycheck. The thought of never seeing a paycheck again is a great shock to many. This is especially true for wives who don't work outside the home. This realization will not manifest itself until after the first or second regular pay period has passed without a paycheck.

Difficulty experienced by one spouse in adjusting to the sudden loss of security can be helped by having that person do the bookkeeping affairs of the business. An understanding of the budgets for both business and personal needs will ease the "no-paycheck shock."

Along with this shock, the new entrepreneur must also allow for a period of time when there will be no profits, and no salaries will be paid from the new venture. It is a rare business that is an instant success and has cash flow from day one.

To cope with this initial cash-flow crunch, all members of the family must pitch in and help control expenses. Don't make the mistake of hiding start-up cash-flow problems from spouses and/or children. If all the family members are aware of the problems, they can contribute in their own way to help ease the situation.

PLAN FOR MAXIMUM CASH

If the opening of the business is scheduled close enough to the termination day of your current job, the drain on cash reserves can be kept minimal. Plan the opening as soon after leaving your job as is possible. Often your final paycheck will be able to bridge the period of time until the business is open.

Do not take a due vacation. Make certain you accumulate as much vacation and sick-leave time as possible. Payment for this accumulated time (if your employer agrees to pay you for it) will aid in the transition from having a regular paycheck to a salary from the new business.

If you have any profit sharing, find out how long it takes to get this money. Some firms take a long time. Do not be caught unprepared.

Once you have quit your job and have gone into business, credit will be very hard to get. Until a business is established, most lenders will shy away from extending credit. Make arrangements for all necessary credit prior to leaving your job. Get credit based on your current employment status. Do *not* discuss your business plans with the lenders. If they think you are quitting your job, it is likely no credit will be advanced.

Raise the limits on all credit cards to their maximum in case you need to use them as a source of cash.

If any major credit purchases are contemplated, do so while you have a fixed income to make the lender happy. Self-employed persons, with new businesses, often have trouble buying on credit.

Visit the local credit agency and request a copy of your credit history. By law, they must allow you to review this information. If you have been denied credit recently, they must give this information to you free of charge. If you have not been denied credit, there will be a small fee charged for this service. Should there be any problems with your credit report, take the time to correct it before credit is needed. The credit reporting agency will tell you how to correct information in your file.

HEALTH INSURANCE

Health insurance is often overlooked when starting a new business. Most people have insurance through group policies where they work.

When that job is terminated, so is the insurance. Today, you can keep your health insurance policy even after you quit.

A new federal law, referred to as COBRA (The Comprehensive Omnibus Budget Reconciliation Act of 1986), allows you to continue with your group coverage for up to eighteen months after you terminate your job, as long as you pay the premiums. It is very important to do this, as individual policies for self-employed people are very expensive and the coverage generally poor.

Most business people don't think twice about insuring their business equipment, the building, or the customers' liability. Often, however, they neglect to insure their most important business asset: family health. *Health claims far surpass any claims for business theft, liability claims, or fire.* Major health problems and their resulting costs are one of the quickest ways to close down a new and struggling business venture.

The human resources office of your current employer can help you with the information you need for continuing your present health care plan. If they can't provide this information, or are unwilling, contact a representative of your current health care plan for details.

FAMILY INVOLVEMENT

A new business venture will affect all family members. This is why each member needs to understand the proposed business and have some input. It doesn't matter whether the husband or the wife or both are leaving their jobs. Changes in the family's habits will result.

Aside from money, there will be many personal changes. Time together with spouses and family members will become scarce. Most new businesses require much more time involvement than regular jobs, and this lack of shared time must be discussed with all family members involved and their understanding solicited.

If the wife is to be the operator of the business, she will need relief from and help with the routine household chores such as cooking, cleaning, and caring for children. Devise a plan so that each member of the family can contribute in some manner to the running of the household.

It is important that each member understand the changes that will result from starting a home-based business and how they can cope with them. Often, change will be unwelcome at first but will be accepted if discussed ahead of time.

If family members are expected to actively work in the business, they should be told how and when, and their cooperation should be voluntary rather than mandated. A simple request for help, with an explanation of the need, will work much better than an edict stating where and when help will be provided.

Consideration should be given to allow the family members, especially children, to have flexible hours so that they can be helpful and still maintain their friends and school activities. Remember, in children's minds fun and friends come first.

If all of these steps have been considered in detail, the transition from a secure job can be made with very little personal and family hassle. With proper planning, the new business venture can be opened on a timely basis and with minimal family stress.

CHAPTER SEVEN

CREATING A BUSINESS PLAN

The creation of your business plan is probably the most important step in setting up your home-based business. By this time you will have chosen the specific home business you want to start and have made preliminary preparations for it. The purpose of the business plan at this point is to help you formulate your overall strategy for the start-up of your venture. We devote a number of pages to this step in order to stress its importance: *Inadequate planning is often the reason for new-business failure.*

When you write your business plan, it helps you take an objective, critical look at your business proposal, free of any emotion or enthusiasm that you may have built up for it; it is a hard look at the facts of the situation. The business plan, when it is completed, can also serve as a kind of operations manual that, if you use it properly, will assist you in managing the business and give you a direction that will lead to success. Finally, your written business plan will serve as a report that you can present to others for the purposes of financing the business. Whether you will be borrowing money from friends and family or a financial institution—if you need to borrow at all—the business plan shows that you are serious about your idea, and your chances of securing start-up capital will be increased.

You can think of your business plan as a management and financial blueprint. You wouldn't and couldn't build a house without a blueprint that specifies the elements, materials, structure, and cost of the building. Likewise, it is inadvisable to begin a business without first defining its structure and specifying the various elements and materials needed to make it successful.

You should plan on writing the business plan yourself; that is, as much as you can write yourself. For certain financial and legal aspects, you may need to consult with an accountant, an insurance agent, and a lawyer. Your need for these outside consultants will probably depend on the size of your home-based operation, and your particular experience or knowledge of the above matters. If your business is small and simple enough, you may be able to complete the business plan by yourself.

Every care should be taken to ensure that your business plan is accurate. To use the blueprint metaphor again, you wouldn't want a house that was constructed with sloppy architectural drawings and inaccurate measurements. An accurate blueprint that has all of its facts straight will give you the most truthful look at your business's chances for success. Your plan must therefore be carefully researched.

The business plan will also clearly explain how your venture will be financed and how you will manage it.

WRITING THE BUSINESS PLAN

The business plan is divided into four main sections: the business description, the marketing plan, the management plan, and the financial plan. This is the basic structure of the plan, and the elements we outline below may or may not be applicable to your business; feel free to alter it to suit your unique needs.

Business Description

Part 1: Business Organization. The following should be typed on your cover page:

Business name _____

Street address _____

Mailing address _____

Telephone number _____

Owner(s) name(s) _____

On the inside pages:

Form of business _____

Here you state the particular form of your business; that is, whether it is a sole proprietorship, a partnership, or a corporation.

Let us digress from our business plan for a moment to explain the three principal forms of business ownership. Once you understand each, you should have no trouble selecting the one that's right for your business.

- Sole Proprietorship—Most people form home businesses as sole proprietorships because it is the easiest business structure to start and the easiest to terminate. As a sole proprietor you have total control of all business assets and are responsible for all debts incurred by the business. You pay taxes as part of your personal tax return by filing a form called Schedule C. (More about this in the chapter about taxes.)
- Partnership—Many people feel more comfortable starting a business with one or more partners, but you should think carefully before doing so. In a business partnership, a partner can make decisions without the approval of other partners, but debts and liabilities extend to *all* partners. In other words, your personal assets can be seized if your business partner makes a costly mistake. A legal partnership-agreement is strongly advised to clarify each partner's role, but even this will not protect you financially. In most cases a sole proprietorship is preferable. If you do choose to become a partner, choose your associate or associates with great care!
- Corporation—Although this is the most complicated business structure to form, it also provides the most personal protection. Simply put, a corporation is a group of people who form a separate legal entity that can operate as one body. The owners, or shareholders, risk only the money they invest. They cannot be held personally responsible for the debts or liabilities of the business unless they sign a separate personal guarantee with a lender. Corporations are required to keep extremely detailed records, and the help of an attorney is usually required. This form of ownership is usually not recommended for new home business owners unless the business has unusual liabilities (a product that could potentially harm a customer, for example).
Now, back to the plan . . .

State of incorporation _____

If you are incorporating, name the state (i.e., Wisconsin) in which you are doing so. In an appendix to the business plan, you should include pertinent documents (if any), such as your partnership agreement, and corporation papers.

Part 2: Business Purpose and Function. In this section you should write an accurate description of your proposed business. In concise language, write your description in narrative form; that is, like a story. The description should include the whats, hows, and whys of your business:

What will be the main activity of the business? State specifically what products or services you will provide. Tell what kind of business it is: retail sales, manufacturing, a service business, etc.

How will you start the business? What's needed here is whether your venture will be a brand-new one, the expansion of one you already operate, the purchase of a going business, or a franchise. Include the actual or proposed start-up date.

Why do you believe your business will succeed? Here is your chance to really promote your idea; give it all the enthusiasm that made you want to start it in the first place. Tell how and why this business will be successful, what is unique about it, how it is better than your competition, and what its niche is in the marketplace.

Next you should detail what particular experience you have in the field of your venture. Include a current résumé. If you have no experience in the field, state how you will acquire the experience or knowledge needed to run the business successfully. Perhaps you can take a training course, for example, or apprentice with a similar business.

The Marketing Plan

This is the main section of your business plan, the one in which you explain the rationale behind your business proposal. To be successful, the business owner must know a lot about the market he or she is about to enter. You will demonstrate your knowledge by providing the results of your market research in this section:

Market Profile
Description of a typical customer:

Age _____

Male, female, or both _____

How many in family _____

Annual family income _____

Location _____

Buying patterns _____

Reason to buy from you _____

Geographic extent of business _____

    (national, state, county, etc.)

Economic extent of business _____

    (single family, average earnings, number of children)

Size of Market
Total number of units or dollars _____

Growing _____ Steady _____ Decreasing _____

If growing, annual rate of growth _____

Competition Profile

No matter what your business is, you are bound to have competition in one form or another. Make a point of thoroughly investigating your competition. Take note of their strengths and weaknesses. The more you know about them, the more likely you are to compete effectively against them. In this section of your business plan, identify your competition, their location, and their products. Also include the following information:

- Your nearest competitors.
- Similarities between their business and yours.
- Describe your unique niche.

- Describe how your product or service is better than the competition's.
- Whether the competition's businesses are growing or declining, and why.
- Any competitive advantages from your business being a home-based one.

Keep in mind that your business can profit by adopting the good practices of the competition and avoiding the negative ones.

To help you see more clearly how your product or service stacks up against the competition, use the following scorecard. For each attribute, write in a score from 0 to 10 for your product or service—0 if the competition's is far superior, 10 if yours is far superior (5 would be an equal score). Add other features that may be applicable to your business.

Feature
Price   _____
Performance   _____
Durability   _____
Versatility   _____
Speed/accuracy   _____
Ease of operation or use   _____
Ease of maintenance or repair   _____
Ease or cost of installation   _____
Size or weight or color   _____
Appearance, styling, or packaging   _____
                              Total Points: _____

If your total point score is less than 60, you may not have enough of an edge over your competition with your present line of products or services. Find ways to strengthen them, then try the scorecard again.

Market Penetration. Estimate what percentage of the market for your business you believe you will be able to win. To figure this, fill out the following:

1. Total market in units or dollars   _____
2. Your estimated planned volume   _____

3. Amount your volume will add to total market   _____
4. Subtract line 3 from line 2   _____
    Line 4 indicates the amount of volume you must be able to win away from your competition in order to see some success.

Pricing and Sales Terms. Explain how you will price your product or service. Knowing how to price is vital for success. Information and formulas on how to arrive at a correct price can be found in Chapter 11 of this handbook. Very basically, however, your costs and expenses should never exceed your selling price. If you know that your product is far superior to your competition's, then you may be able to charge a premium price. If you're going head to head with them, however, a comparable price is recommended. Call on your competitors as a customer and find out all you can about pricing.

Sales Plan. Explain what method of sales you will use: direct sales or mail order.

In direct sales, logically enough, you will be selling your product or service directly to the customer, either in person or by phone. Businesses in this category would include a small retail shop in your home, door-to-door sales, and party-plan sales. You might be a distributor for other companies' product lines or you might be running a franchise.

Mail order is often an ideal way to sell from your home. Through catalogs, flyers, and advertisements, you sell your product or service without direct contact with your customers. All transactions are done by mail (unless you take orders by phone).

Advertising Plan. Detail how you will let the world know about your new business. You don't need to have any elaborate advertising campaign—you probably wouldn't be able to afford it anyway. But you must have some idea of how you are going to communicate your presence to the public. Most home businesses, which are generally very small businesses, do little advertising. Perhaps they have a listing in the Yellow Pages or place an ad in the local shopper papers. And once they are started, word-of-mouth advertising—which may be the best advertising there is—often takes over.

On the other hand, depending on what your business is, you may find that you will have to do a good amount of hustling to get customers, especially if your competition is fierce. In this case you might have to create a direct-mail campaign to potential customers, or even a telephone survey.

In any case, write down what you want your advertising to accomplish. State specific goals, and explain:

- What you will say in your advertising and how you will say it
- What media you will employ
- Your advertising budget
- How you will implement your campaign
- How you will measure its effectiveness

The Management Plan

For the home business operator who is a sole proprietor, this section is very straightforward. In it you must name who will perform what duties in your company. As a sole proprietor, you are the president, and you will most likely do everything yourself.

If your home business will need an employee or two, state what their positions and various duties will be and what you plan to pay them.

If you will be using outside consultants, such as a lawyer or accountant, on a regular basis, explain how often they will be used and approximately how much they will be paid. Next, calculate totals for all salaries, fringe benefits, and payroll taxes for each month of the first year.

In this section you should also explain what types of bank accounts your business will have, and where they are located. Even if you are a sole proprietor, for tax and accounting purposes, you should always keep a separate bank account for your business. Finally, give a brief account of your credit rating. Purchase a copy of your personal credit record from your local credit bureau (such as TRW) and check it to be sure it's accurate.

The Financial Plan

Financial data is important for more than just obtaining a loan if you need one. It is part of your objective analysis. It will determine how much business you must conduct in order to make an acceptable profit. It will identify expenses that might have been overlooked or make it clear that equipment and services that you initially thought were essential will have to be postponed. An important function of the financial plan is that it gives you a standard by which to measure your success. Comparing expenses, income, and profits to the plan will quickly allow you to identify success or the need to overhaul the plan.

Some essential parts of the financial portion of the business plan are:

• Financial sources. Almost any business will require initial funding, even if it is just for paper to write a letter. Financial sources refer not only to banks and investors, but also to your personal bank account.

• Equipment list. Do you have the necessary equipment to carry your business through the initial stages of your plan and, if not, what will be needed? Note that "necessary" is the operative word, and is not the same as "ideal." Obtain only the equipment necessary to accomplish the initial goals of your business plan. For example, a copy machine may be *useful,* but is it *essential?* Can you go to a nearby printshop or library for copies instead?

• Balance sheet. Complete a balance sheet showing assets and liabilities. You will probably be surprised at your own net worth. Properly completed, the balance sheet will prevent early financial disasters, and if it is maintained on a regular basis, will identify financial success or potential trouble areas.

• Break-even analysis. Compare the cost of doing business with the gross receipts. There should be money left over after expenses, including your salary, are accounted for, or you are not making a profit.

• Cash-flow analysis. On a month-by-month basis, for at least a three-year period, determine all expenses, both known and projected, as well as all projected income. After two to three years, there should be a steady increase in profits.

The business plan is a living document. It should be consulted frequently to ensure that your business plans stay on track. It should also be reviewed and revised as necessary on a regular basis.

Your business plan can be three pages or 300 pages, depending on the size and ambition of your venture. It is not the length that counts, but the thought that goes into it.

If you have difficulty developing a plan, an excellent aid is the *How to Write a Business Plan* Project Kit published by the American Institute of Small Business (7515 Wayzata Blvd., Suite 201, Minneapolis, MN 55426). It helps you write every detail of your business plan, step-by-step; it even includes a sample business plan for a delicatessen.

CHAPTER EIGHT

WHERE TO GET START-UP MONEY

The amount of start-up capital necessary to give birth to your home business varies, depending on the type, needs, and size of the business. The start-up process has numerous stages which are listed here by their standard names, along with brief definitions and the amount of ready money you should have available to complete that stage.

Following are the stages for a typical start-up.

INITIAL FUNDING

Money should be available so that your product or idea can be tested for feasibility. Since your small business will most likely be a sole proprietorship (you will be the only owner, will have no partners, and will not sell stock), funding for in-corporation, initial stock issuance and vestment strategies are not needed. However, final development of the business plan is probably the biggest asset you have right now. If you don't have a plan, you have nothing to measure progress against. Start-up expenses for most small businesses in this phase should be between $500 and $2,000.

SEED CAPITAL

Your research has confirmed that there is a need for your product or service, but you need more capital. Bank loans are difficult to obtain for a new business because banks don't like to take risks—especially when they find out you'll be working at home. They will give a loan to an established business, but usually not for start-up. A loan from the Small Business Administration is nearly as difficult to get. The waiting list is a long one, and by the time your loan is approved, you may have lost interest in your business (or someone else will have started a similar one).

Better sources for seed capital are friends and relatives, but before you approach them for a loan, you should investigate other ways to get financing through your own resources. The amounts available from the following sources vary, so make your choice or choices depending on the amount you need:

- A loan on your life insurance
- A second mortgage
- Cash advances on your credit cards and overdraft checking account (be careful; interest rates can be high on the credit cards)
- Selling some of your stocks and bonds
- If you own stock, your stockbroker may be willing to lend you money at a reasonable rate, using your stock as security.

Your financial business plan will give you the best idea of how much money you will, realistically, need to raise. We can't calculate this for you. Besides, costs will vary in different parts of the country for initial inventory (suppliers are reluctant to offer credit to a new enterprise); permit and business-license fees; insurance; advertising; and three to six months' operating expenses.

It is common practice for a new business owner to pay cash for start-up expenses. However, after three or four months you can usually establish normal trade credit with your suppliers.

Most new home business owners will find that the initial capital from their own assets and/or from friends and relatives will be sufficient to start and then operate their business until it becomes profitable. Others, however, with more ambitious projects in mind, will find that additional funding is necessary.

The Informal Venture-Capital Network

Assuming you recognize that you need this extra capital and know approximately how much, the question remains: Where do you get it? There are three major sources:

1. The public equity markets such as the Vancouver Stock Exchange and the Over-the-Counter Market (OTC).
2. Professional venture-capital firms such as Hambrecht & Quist, and U.S. Venture Partners, based in California.
3. The "informal venture-capital network."

Perhaps you've heard of the informal investor network. When venture capital is mentioned, most people think only of professional venture-capital firms. But surveys show that the informal network supplies from three to four times more capital to new and growing firms than is provided by professional venture-capital firms. Some people call informal investors "angels"; others call them "advisory investors," since the entrepreneur gains more than just money from most informal investors (guidance, advice, and a mentor relationship, for example). Below is a characterization of an informal investor, based on demographics. He or she

- is wealthy
- has self-made as opposed to inherited wealth
- is usually in the sixties; almost never below forty
- is usually owner of a "low-tech" business
- usually will invest only within the industry where the money was made.

About 250,000 U.S. millionaires have stated that they invest in new businesses and that they invest anywhere from 10 to 20 percent of their net worth in new businesses. With over a million millionaires in the U.S., and data which indicates that many other wealthy people invest in new and growing businesses, it is safe to assume that there are at least 400,000 informal investors out there.

Do these informal investors usually help run the companies they fund? Research from several sources has consistently indicated that about one out of every five of them contributes nothing but money. The other four engage in levels of activity that range from being on the board of directors to consulting and full-time employment to being part-time employees. Since most of the informal investors are familiar with the industry in which they have invested, their active participation frequently proves to be as valuable (sometimes more so) than their financial contributions.

The next logical question is, where do you find these generous people?

1. The first place to look is among your business associates.
2. Ask business associates to ask their acquaintances.
3. An obvious but frequently overlooked source is your friends.
4. Contact individuals who have been successful in the industry your new firm will address.
5. Don't neglect accountants; many have clients who frequently invest in a new and growing business.
6. Your local banker. However, you will have to really convince him or her of the viability of your company before he or she will recommend you to clients.
7. You may get lucky with an ad in *The Wall Street Journal* classifieds.

Informal investors usually make from one to six investments per year and generally invest from $10,000 to $100,000 in each venture. He or she tends to feel very comfortable when others will also be investing, including professional venture-capital companies. So utilize both sources: you probably will not eliminate any potential investors by doing so.

Informal investors generally expect to lend their money for from three to seven years. Investors in high-tech companies usually get out after a shorter period of time, while low-tech investors tend to hang on longer. High-tech players demand a faster return on their investment because these products quickly become obsolete. These investors also feel that they have to liquidate their stock prior to the next generation of technology, which could depreciate the value of their investment.

Getting a Bank Loan

If you have nowhere to turn for start-up money but a bank, then take your best shot at getting a loan from one, preferably one at which you already have an account. There's a knack to getting a loan, however. Borrowing, like dancing, is somewhat ritualistic. Once you learn the right steps, the process becomes easier and more enjoyable. The following tips will also help to secure loans from venture capitalists—or even your uncle Ned.

Borrowers often let their fear of lenders stand in the way of getting the money they want or need. As a borrower, you must take steps to persuade your banker (or other lender) that you and your home business are good risks for a loan.

Think of Yourself as Creditworthy. How you feel about yourself and your venture comes across loud and clear to others. If you feel you don't really deserve a loan, the loan officer will sense that. A negative attitude can ruin your chances of getting the loan you want.

Put yourself in the lender's shoes. If you were that loan officer, would *you* want to make *you* a loan? If not, it's time for you to determine what you can do to change your negative profile.

Do you have a good credit history? Your banker will check with a local credit-reporting agency. Your credit report is a profile of your payment history with other creditors. If you have a history of paying your creditors on time, your history should be good.

Don't know what's in your credit report? Call your local credit bureau or other credit-reporting agency to find out how to get a copy. You may view your report in person at the credit-reporting agency, or you may order a copy by mail. (Most agencies charge a small fee.)

If you haven't seen a recent copy of your report, you should order one before you approach the lender. Make sure the information in the report is correct. Given the large number of credit reports made daily, mistakes do occur. Your report could accidentally contain information on someone with a name or Social Security number close to yours.

If you find a mistake in your report, you have the right to have the credit-reporting agency reverify the information. If the agency cannot reverify the information, it must remove it from your record. This is particularly helpful to know in case your report includes negative credit information on someone else.

Study your report to see if it contains any information that might need explaining. For example, divorce often wreaks havoc with credit. Maybe you got a divorce four years ago and in the process you or your former spouse fell behind in payments to creditors. For the past three years, however, you have paid your bills on time. Tell the lender about this before he or she has the opportunity to check your credit report. By knowing about the problems ahead of time, the lender will not get any surprises when reading your report. (Note: Lenders don't like surprises.)

Think of a Loan as Money You Want, Not Need, to Borrow. The lender doesn't want to think that you actually need the money. If you truly need it, you probably won't have the ability to repay the loan.

Again, consider the banker's position. He is in charge of making loans. His success in the bank depends on his ability to make loans that will be repaid, with interest. If the bank can't collect the interest and principal payments due on the loan, it loses money. And he, as loan officer, must account for having made a loan that went bad.

As a borrower, you must convince the loan officer that your business will be successful enough to repay the loan. So remember to pay attention to how you ask for the loan: You don't *need* the loan—you *want* the loan.

Write a Cover Letter to the Lender. Before approving a loan, a lender will need the following information:

• How much money do you want to borrow? Determine exactly how much money you will ask to borrow *before* you go to the bank.

• What do you want the money for? Lenders know that if you borrow money without a legitimate business reason in mind, you may squander it. Later, you will probably have nothing to show for it, and may have trouble repaying the loan. Keep in mind that lenders make business loans for specified purposes. Some lenders are more restrictive than others in approving business loans. Some acceptable purposes for a business loan include the following:

    Buying an interest in another business
    Financing new equipment
    Repairing business equipment
    Paying for current operations

Building up inventory
Modernizing existing equipment or buildings
Financing accounts receivable
Paying for advertising or sales promotion
Expanding existing product lines
Enlarging production
Saving money by increasing operating efficiency

• How long will it take you to repay? This depends on the amount you borrow. The bank may want to make a 90-, 120-, or 180-day loan. Or, if the loan qualifies, you may have the option of repaying in monthly installments, amortized over a period of years. You may want to call the bank to find out what kinds of loans qualify for different paybacks.

• How will you repay the loan? If you are already in business, your primary income source for repaying the loan will probably be your profits. The lender will ask for copies of your federal income tax returns for the past three years. If you are just starting a business, you must show a current source of income for paying off the loan.

Perhaps you are starting your business on a part-time basis or continuing in your present job for a while? If so, the lender will ask for your latest pay stub. This will establish that you do have an income source for paying off the loan. If that income source fails, how else could you repay it? The lender wants to know how secure the loan will be. Change is inevitable, and circumstances beyond your control can cut off your income source.

Suppose you become disabled or business falls off. Or you quit your present job before your new business can show a profit. How will you repay the debt that you owe the bank? The lender will want to know, so prepare to discuss what assets can serve as a secondary source of repayment. You might have stocks, bonds, or other assets which you could sell.

Now that you know which questions the loan officer will ask, write a cover letter to the lender that includes the answers. Keep the letter brief and to the point. A typical letter might read:

Dear Lender:

I would like to borrow $5,000 on a 120-day note to purchase inventory for the Christmas season. I anticipate a holiday season of brisk sales, and I will repay the loan from my profits. In the event of less-than-spectacular sales, I can draw on my savings account as a secondary source of repayment.

I enclose a copy of my last three federal tax returns, operating statement, and evidence of my savings account balance.

Thank you for your consideration.

Sincerely,
John Smith

The bank will have its own application form which you must complete. If you can, stop by ahead of time to pick up the form. Take it home with you and fill it out at your leisure. Be sure to answer all questions. Make sure the completed application is neat and legible. Attach it and your supporting financial information to your cover letter. Then visit your lender, knowing that by being prepared you will make a favorable impression.

If your bank is not willing to make the loan, ask why. If the bank simply is not making the kind of loan that you are requesting, shop around. Visit another bank, and another, until you find one that will make the loan. Who knows, you may even find better rates. Keep in mind that persistence pays off.

10 TIPS FOR GETTING YOUR LOAN APPROVED

1. Keep in mind that to stay in business banks need to make loans. Do not be afraid to ask for one. That's what the loan officer wants you to do.
2. Come to the loan interview prepared. Bring a completed loan application, copies of financial documentation, and your cover letter. Try to anticipate any question the loan officer might ask you.
3. Don't take an apologetic attitude. Present yourself as an entrepreneur who can and will repay the loan.
4. Dress in a professional manner for the interview. This is a business transaction, so treat it as such.
5. Don't stretch the truth in your loan application. The lender can easily check many of the facts on your application.

6. Type all your loan documents. Handwritten documents look unprofessional.
7. Don't push the loan officer for a decision. Doing so might result in a no.
8. Be confident. An attitude of confidence enhances your chance of getting the loan.
9. Keep trying one lender after another until you get your loan.
10. Remember that the first loan is usually the hardest to get.

For more information, purchase or check your library for the following publications: *Venture Capital Sources.* Forum Publishing Co., 383 East Main St., Centerport, NY 11721; *2001 Sources of Financing for Small Business* by Herman Holtz. Arco Publishing, 215 Park Avenue South, New York, NY 10003; *The Small Business Guide to Borrowing Money* by Richard L. Ruben and Philip Goldberg. McGraw-Hill Book Co., 1221 Avenue of the Americas, New York, NY 10020; *A Handbook of Small Business Finance.* Superintendent of Documents, U.S. Government Printing Office, Washington, D.C. 20402; *The Arthur Young Guide to Raising Venture Capital* by G. Steven Burrill and Craig T. Norback. Tab Books Inc., Blue Ridge Summit, PA 17294-0850; *Guide to Venture Capital Sources* edited by Stanley E. Pratt. Capital Publishing Co., PO Box 348, Two Laurel Avenue, Wellesley Hills, MA 02181; *How to Finance Your Small Business With Government Money: SBA and Other Loans* by Rick S. Hayes and John C. Howell. Ronald Press, a division of John Wiley & Sons, 605 Third Avenue, New York, NY 10158-0012.

CHAPTER NINE

START-UP BASICS

CHOOSE A NAME

LARRY LEMON'S USED CARS. Would you buy a used car from this man? SPIKE MAHONEY'S BALLET SCHOOL. What is wrong with the names of these businesses? The importance of the name of a new company cannot be overlooked, but surprisingly, it often is. The name that you give to your new business can significantly affect the business's chances of success.

In a hypothetical scenario, let's suppose that you wish to start a home-based mail-order business that sells yellow pencils in Centertown, Iowa, and your name is John Doe. In all the hours that you toiled on this project, however, you never once considered naming your business, so at the eleventh hour you settle on DOE YELLOW PENCIL SALES.

What's wrong with that? Everything! Each word possesses a negative connotation that could hurt your business. The word "Doe" divulges to potential customers that the firm is a one-man operation. "Yellow" limits your business. What if you are later able to sell red, green, and rainbow-colored pencils? "Pencil" has the same liability. You may someday wish to stock other office products such as pens, paper, and paper clips. "Sales" repels business people immediately. The word has unpleasant connotations and alerts consumers to the probability that anything you handle has been marked up at least once from the factory price.

What would have been a better name? If your business is strictly local, how about CENTERTOWN OFFICE SUPPLY COMPANY? If you plan to make many out-of-area sales, an expansive geographical name such as IOWA OFFICE SUPPLIES or a vague but nonetheless impressive name such as IMPERIAL OFFICE SUPPLY COMPANY would have worked better.

For the naming process, you need more than an engineer's understanding of your product, and more than a manager's grasp of your company's strengths. You must be able to distance yourself from what you're naming, enough to find out how your customers perceive your business, what they want from it, and what it can do to fill the needs they believe they have. Try to be ever-conscious of your customers' demands; let the name of your company serve your customers as well as instill confidence in them.

To begin the process, gather a pool of information concerning your company. First, describe what you are naming. What services will your business provide? Maybe you specialize in iced goods. The name JUST-ICE might serve you well. Set a marketing strategy that will isolate the types of people you want your name to appeal to. If you ran an in-home hair-care service, you probably would not appeal to the older market you wish to reach with a name like PUNK ROCK HAIR KUTTERZ.

Make a list of the names that you like and dislike. Use this list as a reference guide, and explain what appeals to you about your favorites and what repels you from liking other names. Write down your competitors' names, and see where they fit onto your list. Can your business's name compete with your competitors'?

After you have gathered some pertinent information, you can start toying with ideas for the name of your business. Keep in mind that there are still many things to consider when naming a company that you might not ordinarily have contemplated. For example, some names are very hard to trademark. Other names might infringe on other companies' trademarks. Some words that were once widely used in business names are now considered cliché. Here are eleven hints that concern the naming of a new company; use them to eliminate certain ideas which might have otherwise caused you heartache or to hit upon a new idea you had not yet considered:

1. Geographical names usually work best. If your customers live in one town, name your company after that town, or a geographical name peculiar to that area, such as NEW YORK WIDGET or MANHAT-TAN WIDGET. These immediate associations will have a great impact on your customers.

2. Companies that operate over a large area would best be served by names that imply vastness, including: AMERICAN, STANDARD, INTERNATIONAL, GLOBAL, NATIONAL, UNIVERSAL, STATE, NORTHERN, EASTERN, WESTERN, SOUTHERN, GULF, AT-LANTIC, PACIFIC, INNER-MOUNTAIN, ACME, UNITED, CON-SOLIDATED, AMALGAMATED, SENTINEL, and so forth. These names possess an unlimited reach that is quite potent.

3. Avoid initials. Companies with names like AAA GADGET or TKSRBL COMPANY lack personality and are easily ignored by poten-tial customers. Unless one considers . . .

4. Acronyms (words formed out of initials, such as "scuba" and "radar") are clever and imaginative. This wit won't be lost on your customers. And furthermore . . .

5. Names with initials, in the hands of a good commercial artist, can be transformed into an attractive logo. If your company was named TWIN TOWERS, for example, both of the T's could be drawn in a very elongated manner.

6. Avoid names that resemble the names of larger corporations. When the INTERNATIONAL ARMAMENTS COMPANY consis-tently referred to itself as INTERARMCO, it was successfully sued by the ARMCO STEEL CORPORATION.

7. Avoid the timeworn and hackneyed word "Enterprises." Look in big-city telephone directories and you will discover hundreds of firms with names like DOE ENTERPRISES or JD ENTERPRISES. A hand-ful are medium-sized or large firms, but many are kitchen-table opera-tions whose owners tacked "Enterprises" on their names so that they could change the direction of the company at any time. The word "Enterprises" often connotes a falsehood and dishonesty which should be avoided.

8. Avoid using your family name in the name of the firm. If it is small, it hampers the company's chances of becoming big. If it is big, then it is simply archaic. There are many exceptions to this rule, but it is still sound advice in today's business world.

9. Make sure that the name of the company has something to do with the type of product you sell. Whereas it might be true that the Coca-Cola Company has been very successful in its ownership of the seemingly unrelated Columbia Pictures, it would be very unlikely for you to meet similar success trying to sell corndogs with a name like Michael's Mufflers.

10. Give a sense of balance and rhythm to the name of your company. Avoid the long-winded (INTERNATIONAL BUCKET & SHOVEL CONSOLIDATED MANUFACTURING, INC.), the obscure (XYZ, Inc.), or the complicated (KR & W, CNO/XYZ & SON, PTE. LTD.).

11. Make sure your name conforms to the industry standards that have been set. Add "tronics" to an electronic firm, but not to a grocery store.

Selecting a name is a very personal and creative activity; you are the one who has to live with the name you choose. It's your money that will promote it and build its reputation, and it's your name that will be associated with it. A solid name can help give you a head start. A clever name is a form of free advertising. A stodgy name will forever be a hindrance to your success.

REGISTER A FICTITIOUS NAME

If the business name you choose is different from your name, even if it's Jane Doe Enterprises, you must file an assumed (or fictitious) name certificate with your county.

Go to your county clerk and say that you want to register such a name. There will be a form or two to fill out, and then your business name will have to be checked against records of names of already-existing businesses to avoid duplication. Either the county clerk's office will conduct this search or you will be required to do it yourself. It's really quite simple. The office will have a card file or computer file of existing business names arranged alphabetically. You merely check the file to see if there is already a business having the exact name you have chosen. If not, you're in luck. If there is, fall back on your second choice and check again.

The fee for registering a fictitious name varies from state to state, but it ranges from $10 to $40. You will also probably have to have the forms you filled out notarized. A notary public is often on the premises for this purpose, and notarization may cost you another $5 or so.

Be sure to complete this step before you invest in expensive stationery and brochures. It costs little to file your name, and it protects your business from being used by someone else in the county.

CHECK ON ZONING RESTRICTIONS

Find out how your property is zoned—either commercial, agricultural, or residential—then call City Hall and ask what regulations apply to home businesses in that zone. Also, if you rent or live in a condominium, check the lease or homeowners' association rules to be certain a home business is allowed.

Generally, if you do not annoy your neighbors with excess noise, odors, and traffic, you will not be deterred from running a business at home. The neighbors may not even be aware of the business, but it is necessary to know exactly what you can and can't do before you start. This is important should any problems or questions arise later.

GET AN IDENTIFYING NUMBER

If you are the sole proprietor of the business and have no employees, you may use either your Social Security number or an Employee Identification Number (EIN) as the business number on official forms. If you have employees, or the business is set up as a partnership or corporation, you must obtain an EIN. To do this, complete IRS Form SS-4 (Application for Employer Identification Number) and file it with the nearest IRS Center.

OBTAIN A SALES TAX PERMIT

If the product or service you sell is taxable, you need a state sales tax permit. Call the local tax agency, explain the type of business you have and what you sell, and ask if you need to collect sales tax. If you do, they will send you the necessary information and forms to complete. You also use this tax number when you purchase items for resale.

OBTAIN LICENSES AND PERMITS

It's very important not to overlook any license or permit that may be necessary for your particular business. For example, some cities and counties require a general business license, and most have special laws regarding the preparation and sale of food.

Call City Hall to find out what is needed for your particular business. In addition, chambers of commerce provide information on city, county, and state licenses and permits.

OPEN A BUSINESS CHECKING ACCOUNT

You will need a separate checking account for your business. Since some of your customers will be paying you by check made out to your business name, a checking account under that name must be established. Call several banks to find out what services they offer, and what minimum balance, if any, must be maintained to avoid paying a service charge. Also ask about credit card service if you plan to offer this convenience to your customers. Bank fees can be significant, so shop around for the best deal.

If your personal checking account is with a credit union, see if it can also provide a separate business account. When you open the account, you may need to show the fictitious-name certificate and business license.

Finally, investigate obtaining a credit card in the business's name. If this is not possible, set aside a personal credit card to use for business expenses.

SET UP RECORD-KEEPING SYSTEMS

Put together a simple and effective bookkeeping system with an $8\frac{1}{2} \times$ 11-inch three-ring binder, columnar pad sheets, and twelve pocket dividers from the office supply store. For each month, set up columnar sheets for income and expenses. Use a pocket divider for each month's receipts, bank statement, deposit tickets, and canceled checks.

In addition, an automobile log for business mileage and a filing system for correspondence, invoices, supplier catalogs, client records, etc., are two other useful aids.

For more information on record-keeping, see IRS Publication #583, *Information for Business Taxpayers.*

CHECK IRS REQUIREMENTS

If you comply with basic IRS guidelines, you can deduct a percentage of normal household expenses (mortgage interest, taxes, insurance, utilities, repairs, etc.) as a business expense. See Chapter 17 for more detailed information, and IRS Publication #587, *Business Use of the Home.*

Also, become familiar with these IRS forms: Schedule SE (Computation of Social Security Self-Employment Tax) and Schedule 1040-ES (Estimated Tax for Individuals). Depending on circumstances, you may have to file them.

CHECK OUT THE POST OFFICE AND UPS

Using a post office box as the business address downplays the fact you are home-based. It also prevents customers from dropping in at all hours.

While looking into box rental, ask for information on the various postal rates, particularly bulk rate, if you plan to do large or specialized mailings. If you mail many packages, check out United Parcel Service (UPS), as it is less expensive than the Post Office.

PURCHASE THE NECESSARY INSURANCE

Check with your homeowners insurance agent about a rider for your existing policy or the need for a separate business policy. Also make sure you have adequate personal and product-liability coverage. Shop around, as each company has different rules regarding home businesses.

To save money on medical insurance, join an association and participate in their group plan. One such body is the National Association for the Self-Employed; they can be reached at 800-527-5504.

SET UP A KEOGH PLAN

Go to your bank and inquire how you can set up a Keogh Plan for your home business. A Keogh Plan allows you to set a certain amount of your income money aside for retirement purposes. This money is tax deferred; that is, you won't be taxed on it until you reach retirement age, when your taxes will be much less.

CHAPTER TEN

SET PRIORITIES, MANAGE YOUR TIME— AND YOUR SPOUSE, CHILDREN, AND HOUSEHOLD CHORES

Distractions may be unavoidable when you work at home, but they don't have to cause a problem. When you take off for an occasional afternoon outing, it is always possible to make up for lost time by working longer hours the next day. The freedom to determine when and how long you will work is one of the best reasons for being your own boss. But watch out. You are apt to be lured away from your work enough times—especially around the holidays—to seriously endanger your profits.

If you think that willpower has nothing to do with home business, you are missing out on an effective self-improvement tool that can help you get the job done. Until now, no one has been able to explain exactly what willpower is, and how it can help us do exactly what we are supposed to do. *Willpower Guide* (Rise Personal Development) by William Eddy is a book that is subtitled "Never Give Up." Eddy teaches us exactly what willpower is, and includes step-by-step techniques that will help us take advantage of opportunities and convert them into concrete achievements.

Eddy knows about willpower. A former juvenile delinquent, alcoholic, and drug addict, Eddy rehabilitated himself by assuming full responsibility for his own behavior. He has since spent twenty-seven years helping alcoholics become constructive, contented people. Throughout the years he became convinced that willpower is more than just the determination to get what you want. He realized that it had six essential components that must be coordinated in order to be most effective. They are:

1. Concentrate on goals and personal principles. To be successful, we all need to clearly determine our long-range goals and then devise a step-by-step plan to help us achieve them. It is necessary to give our full attention to this gradual process and use personal commitment to help us adhere to our plan.

2. Your goals should be very specific. Don't say: "I will earn more money next year." Instead, say: "I will acquire five additional clients next year." Then determine each small step necessary to achieve this goal. If you derive personal satisfaction from each achievement, you will gain the incentive you need to proceed on course.

3. Control of habits and impulses. The way you control your living patterns can control your destiny. Eddy says our habits will take us either toward our goals or away from them; our habits will help us live up to our principles or cause us to violate them. By gradually developing constructive habits, we can turn our weaknesses into strengths.

4. If you are having trouble concentrating on work during your regular hours, develop a new routine. For example, you could begin work two hours earlier each day to gain momentum before the distractions begin. At first, it might be difficult to get up early, but your willpower can get you through this difficult period of transition. Eventually, rising early will become a positive habit that won't require much effort on your part.

5. Flexibility. Circumstances change, and it may be necessary to find new ways to reach your goals. If conditions are beyond your control, complaining is a waste of precious time. Instead, try to do the best you can with what you have.

It is necessary to make goals when you start your home business, but as you work, your ideas and business will evolve and you will begin to see that some of your original goals have become outdated. Goal-setting is an ongoing process, and you must remain flexible enough to revise your plan as necessary.

6. Persistence. The process of growth can be painful and filled with obstacles. You will not fail until you give up, so learn to accept each new challenge and develop enough willpower to persist when others do not.

Wanting a successful home business is not enough to make it happen. Rejection and disappointment are part of the growth process, and only those who are willing to overcome obstacles will ever have a chance of getting what they want.

When you add some basic time-management techniques to your newfound willpower, you can do your work more efficiently. You don't have to follow a nine-to-five routine to be productive, but you do have to establish your own personal schedule to safeguard your work from unwanted distractions and interruptions. Try to work the same hours every day, and make a daily work plan to follow. Keep a master list of projects that need to be completed, then prioritize this list by assigning a #1 or #2 or #3 next to each entry. Then choose a few items to complete each day. Try to handle related items together, schedule all telephone calls for the same time, and check off each entry as you complete it.

TENDING TO SPOUSE, CHILDREN, AND HOUSEHOLD CHORES

This section applies to women or men who work in the home and must also contend with their other job: domestic engineer—otherwise known as being a housewife, or, less commonly, househusband. Taking care of the home is arguably one of the most challenging, exhausting, and fulfilling careers of all. It is because of this importance that we take time to explain how to be both housewife (or househusband) and successful home business manager.

Increasingly, men are being househusbands while their wives go off to work. This is especially true if the husband has a home business and must also attend to the traditional male household chores: lawn cutting, car maintenance, and general household repairs.

In some instances, of course, both husband and wife are home to run the business. In this case, both must share the responsibilities of business management and home management.

Here is what one mother who works at home says:

The day began calmly but quickly turned to chaos, and it seemed as if all my troubles came in pairs. My two children, ages six and eleven, were home with the flu. Because their rooms are on opposite sides of the house, and sore throats prevented them from calling out, each child had a bell to use when they needed my attention. Their simultaneous ringing took no heed of my two impending deadlines, the two telephones constantly ringing (more bells) and two important appointments that had to be canceled. Yes, I am a homeworking mother, and I love every minute of it—even on days like this.

Working at home is one way for parents to manage all of their diverse responsibilities in the same place. Is it easy? No. Is it possible? Yes! It works for thousands of parents. With the right kind of support, organization, and commitment it can work for you too.

BEFORE YOU BEGIN

Babies who are born into a household with one or both parents working at a home business grow up expecting to see them spend at least part of their day doing business, and instinctively learn to occupy themselves during that time. But when you start your home business after your children have developed preconceived expectations of you, you have to ease into your new role. It is a good idea to plant the seeds of your work/ parenting relationship long before you actually begin your home business. Spend some time each day reading a book, typing a letter, or paying bills and ask your children to respect mommy's or daddy's time. They will begin to view you as a loving parent who also has interests and responsibilities that are separate from their wants and needs. Once that happens, it will be easier for you to gain their support and understanding as you begin to work at home.

You will be better able to cope if you separate your work area from your family's space right from the beginning. As we have pointed out, if you have an extra room that can be turned into an office, it will be easier to make sure that little hands never touch important papers, but an entire room is not essential. Choose a corner, a large closet, any space you can call your own. Set firm guidelines from the beginning: No one touches anything on your desk or worktable without asking first.

If you will be making or receiving business phone calls, have a separate telephone line installed for your business, and make sure you have a hold or mute button on your telephone. Answer that phone using your business name, and put an answering machine on when you cannot answer it yourself. There is nothing more disconcerting to a prospective client than hearing a three-year-old on the other end of the line.

IN BUSINESS

Once you have established your home business and your family accepts the fact that you are a homeworking parent, you will have to continue your careful planning. You will soon find out that working at home is not the answer to all of your child-care problems. The ages of your children, the type of business you are running, and your personal experiences will help you determine exactly how many hours you can expect to work throughout the day.

Mothers of very young children usually put in a few hours of work during nap times and while "Sesame Street" is on TV. If your business is generating enough income, you can hire an assistant who will help with the children and do some clerical work for part of the day. Even though you are probably working at home to spend more time with your children, there is no shame in asking for and getting the help you need to make it all work. Even if a babysitter is caring for your children while you are working in your office, you are still there, able to oversee all of their activities and take frequent hug breaks. Parents who are away in an unseen office outside the home would certainly envy your accessibility.

Don't despair if your income is too low to pay for outside help. If you have a supportive and understanding spouse, he or she can take care of dinner and the children's needs while you work, then help you with your business after the children have gone to bed for the night. When you use the years when the children are little to start your business, you have the opportunity to lay a strong foundation. Then your business can grow right along with your children. By the time they are in school all day, you will have a business that is ready for your full-time attention.

SECRETS OF SUCCESS

All parents working at home need to explore the best ways to make business compatible with raising children. Each parent will develop his or her own techniques in response to the particular needs of the family. Here are ten proven ways to have happy children and enough time to work at home:

1. Explain your business to your children. Talk about some of the problems you are facing, and share good news when it happens. Even the youngest children will understand that you are including them in your activities, and the result will be greater cooperation.

2. Create regular business hours in which your children expect you to be working and your clients will know they can reach you. Children find it easier to accept any activity that occurs at approximately the same time each day. When work hours are always followed by a child-centered activity, you will feel less guilty and your children will develop the necessary patience. If possible, divide your work hours. For example, work two hours in the morning, two hours in the afternoon, and two more hours after the kids' bedtime.

3. Create firm guidelines for your children to follow during work hours, such as: (a) no interruptions during business calls unless it is an emergency; (b) use earphones for music and keep the television volume down low. Some homeworking mothers post their rules on the office door. Once your children realize that you mean business, they will do what is expected of them.

4. Be accessible. Let your children know that most of the time you can be interrupted if necessary. Stopping for a hug, to comb a doll's hair, fix a dart gun, or to admire a drawing maintains a connection between you and your children, and these activities take a minimum amount of time. Make sure you leave snacks and interesting activities out for your kids before you begin to work.

5. When you are doing work that keeps your hands busy but does not require concentration, use that time to sing songs, tell stories, help with homework, or any other verbal activity that you can do with your child.

6. If you have a preschooler, set up a small replica of your work area nearby for your little one to work in. You can collect discarded mail, magazines, and other papers for cutting and pasting. A garage-sale typewriter and a toy telephone will complete your child's miniature office.

7. Keep a special collection of (quiet) toys which stay in your office. Your child will consider it a treat to be able to play with them while you work.

8. Tape record your child's favorite storybooks so that they can be played at will.

9. Give your children age-appropriate jobs to do for you. Little ones can stuff envelopes and put stamps on them. Older children can sort mail and do filing. Make your children feel that they are making a valuable contribution, try not to criticize, and have fun with them while they work with you. Before you know it, you will look forward to their participation.

10. Share your profits. When you make an important sale or if the mail brings in some long-awaited checks, buy your child a gift or go out for dinner in a favorite restaurant. This will show them that they can benefit directly from your work, and they will want to do everything possible to help you succeed in your home business.

CHAPTER ELEVEN

HOW TO PRICE YOUR PRODUCT OR SERVICE

Jack Perkins started his home-based mail-order business with high hopes and a good product, but with little understanding of the mechanics of the business. His product was a new and handy piece of camping gear that he could make at home. Before writing up his first ad, he toured the sporting goods stores to find out the prices of similar items at the retail level. The prices averaged $5.95, and he reasoned that because his gadget was new and superior, he could charge a bit more. So he decided on a price of $7.50, put together a couple of magazine ads, and sat back to wait for the orders to come in. They came, and plenty of them. However, soon he was out of business and deep in debt.

Dick West, on the other hand, went into business with a home and office cleaning service. For every job, Dick gave an estimate based on the cost of his own labor ($10 an hour)—$3 more than he had ever made as a salaried employee. Advertising and word-of-mouth recommendations brought him a lot of work, but in a few months' time he was worse off financially than when he started, and he was wondering desperately what went wrong.

Jack and Dick both fell into one of the big pitfalls in business: unscientific pricing. Ideally, a price should meet three requirements:

- It should match the competition.
- It should be attractive to your potential customers.
- It should earn a profit.

Jack allowed his price to be set by the competition, not by his own needs. Dick engineered his prices on the basis of direct costs, adding what he haphazardly estimated as a margin of profit—the extra $3 per hour above his usual salary. Neither set a price based on dollars-and-cents facts. They both kept busy, but they couldn't make money, and eventually their businesses buckled. *The right price for a product or service is one of the essential blocks in a solid business structure.* The wrong price tag, however, is like a ticket to disaster.

The right selling price must cover three elements:

1. *Direct Cost*—the money you must spend to perform a specific job or sell a specific product. In a retail business, for example, the direct cost of an item would be its wholesale price plus the cost of advertising that specific item. In a service business, the direct cost of a job would be the materials and labor for that specific job.

2. *Indirect Costs*—the money you have to spend to stay in business. This includes things like utilities, supplies, management and clerical costs, and general advertising. To set an intelligent price, you must distribute these costs appropriately over all the products and services you sell.

3. *Profit on Investment*—this is the element most often overlooked or underestimated by beginners in business. Profit is money you should make in addition to a reasonable salary for your services. If your prices don't allow for profit as well as for the cost of your labor, then obviously you'll never make more money working for yourself than working for somebody else.

ANALYZING THE COSTS

Setting a price without analyzing costs is like trying to negotiate the Sea of Sargasso with a compass from a package of Cracker Jack. Let's examine what happened to Jack when he tried to set a mail-order price by casing the retail competition.

Jack started with two ads: a small one in a mass-circulation men's magazine that cost $550 and a larger one in a small-circulation hobby magazine that cost $450. He got 160 orders from the first ad and 95 from the second, for a total of 255 orders at $7.50 each. Not bad for a beginner.

Then Jack started to fill the orders, and ran into trouble. The cost of materials for making the gadget was $2.70 each. In addition, to produce large quantities of these gadgets he had to hire some teenagers to help. He paid them $2.80 an hour, and they averaged four pieces each hour. Add the $2.70 materials cost for each item with a 70¢ labor cost, and the total per item comes to $3.40.

With this kind of wholesale cost, a retailer could make out very well on a $7.50 selling price. However, Jack still had to add the special costs of mail order. Each order had cost him $3.92 in advertising. In addition, without counting his own labor, packing and mailing cost him 84¢ per item. So at this point, the total cost was $8.16 per piece, and he was losing 66¢ on each sale ($165 on his first ad campaign). Now, if Jack had some other products, related items that could have brought him some repeat business from his 255 costly customers, he might have come out okay in the long run. However, since his whole operation consisted of a single product, all his costs were direct costs, but they were massive.

Of course, mail order is a special kind of business, with special pricing requirements. Experienced mail-order operators will rarely handle any product that they can't sell at four times its wholesale cost, and some don't feel safe unless the product can take an eight-to-one markup. *In any business, even one where costs are low, the basic relationship between costs and price is a major factor in success.*

Consider Dick West's cleaning business, a typical one-man enterprise. Dick invested $2,400 in equipment that allows him to do a thorough job very quickly. He also bought a used truck for $3,800. His total investment: $6,200. His indirect costs are relatively low because he works out of his home; they amount to about $180 per month. Under direct costs, he has only the low cost of materials plus his own labor.

Dick is charging $10 per hour for his service, which seems like a lot to him because the most he ever earned as a salaried employee was $7 per hour. In an average thirty-day month, he puts in 192 working hours, just as he did when he was working for somebody else. But he can work on jobs only for about six hours a day. The rest of the time is spent in transportation, taking calls, scheduling, and billing. In an average month, then, he has 144 money-producing hours at $10 per hour. His total income is $1,440 per month, from which he must subtract $180 in indirect costs and $100 in materials. He clears $1,160 per month, considerably less than the $1,344 he earned in an average month on a $7 per hour salary. And that was before he invested $6,200 in his own business. Clearly, his price is wrong.

FINDING FULL COSTS

Dick needs a price scale that will offer a more reasonable profit. The first step in finding out the right price is determining the full cost of doing business per month, including the indirect costs and the owner's labor. In the example below, we list Dick's labor cost at his previous salary—the very least he can afford to clear and still make it worthwhile for him to stay in business for himself.

Indirect Expenses	
Truck maint., fuel, insurance	$ 80
Telephone answering service	30
Ads in local newspapers	50
Labor	1,344
Direct Costs	
Miscellaneous	20
Materials	100
Total	$ 1,624

The next step in determining a reasonable price is figuring out how much it costs to provide the service during each hour of productive work. In this case: $1,624 (monthly cost) divided by 144 (productive hours per month) = $11.28.

In short, by charging $11.28 per hour for each job, Dick could earn exactly as much as he did before he went into business. This is the full cost of producing the service, and the very least he can afford to charge without taking a loss. It's hardly a fair return on his investment, however, and on his growing managerial skills. In addition, there ought to be some profit on his sales. Suppose it's 10 percent, a fairly low but

typical profit in service businesses. In the language of pricing, a net
profit of 10 percent means that the cost complement is 90 percent (that
is, 100 percent minus the net profit). To figure a selling price that will
include this 10 percent profit, use this formula:

$$\frac{\text{Cost of service per hour}}{\text{Cost complement} \times 100} = \text{Selling price}$$

In the case of Dick's business, the arithmetic works out like this:

$$\frac{\$11.28}{90 \times 100} = \$12.53$$

To make a decent income, plus a fair profit on his investment, Dick
should be charging $12.53 per hour for his service.

To find the actual full cost of each of the services, the cost analysis
breaks down the indirect expenses and distributes them for each of the
services. The cost analysis/cost complement formula can be used to
find the right selling price in any business, even a complicated one.

HIDDEN EXPENSES

Suppose, for example, that you have a desktop publishing business
which you operate with the help of two assistants. A large part of the
business is designing and printing flyers, but this service is mainly a
bait that pulls in bigger jobs, such as brochures and newsletters. On
flyer jobs, materials are extra and quoted separately for each job, and
you want to keep labor prices low without losing money on the jobs.
The bigger jobs, though, are supposed to pay off your heavy investment
in equipment and earn a profit for the business; quoted prices for these
jobs must include the cost of materials.

As before, the first step in pricing is finding the full cost for each
service. Since there is more than one service, you have to estimate how
much time, space, and overhead each one uses, so the costs can be
properly distributed. For instance, the floor space required for producing flyers is only one-fourth as much as the space needed for the bigger
jobs, so rent costs are distributed proportionately. Your advertising

mostly pitches the bigger jobs, so cost is distributed proportionately, too.

DISTRIBUTION OF EXPENSES

	Total	Flyers	Other jobs
Indirect Expenses			
Rent	$ 500.00	$ 100.00	$ 400.00
Asst. #1 salary	550.00	350.00	200.00
Other overhead	400.00	200.00	200.00
(insurance, licenses, utilities, etc.)			
Direct Expenses			
Your salary	1,300.00	300.00	1,000.00
Asst. #2 salary	850.00	600.00	250.00
Material	700.00	—	700.00
Total	$4,300.00	1,550.00	2,750.00

The next step, again, is to find out the cost per productive working hour, this time for each of the services. In an average working month with 192 working hours, Service 1 is producing 90 percent of the time, or about 173 hours. Dividing total costs by total productive hours:

$$\$1,550 \div 173 = \$8.96$$

Thus, by charging $8.96 per hour, plus material costs for flyers, you can meet your actual expenses for producing them. However, since equipment costs are high, you should add 10 percent net profit to this figure (beware: this won't give you a large profit either). Now, use the cost-complement formula:

$$\frac{\$8.96 \times 100}{90} = \$9.96$$

The price for flyers, then, should be $9.96 per hour plus materials.

Let's find the price for Service 2, which produces 85 percent of the time, or about 163 hours. Dividing total costs by total productive hours, you get the cost per productive hour:

$$\$2{,}750 \div 163 = \$16.87$$

In the desktop publishing business, where investment in equipment and software is high, a 20 percent net profit is reasonable and usually competitive, so the cost complement here is 80:

$$\frac{\$16.87 \times 100}{80} = \$21.09$$

So for a fair price and a reasonable profit, you'd charge $21.09 per hour for the bigger jobs.

ADJUSTING TO CIRCUMSTANCES

By using cost analysis and the cost-complement formula, it's possible to find the right price for almost any service or product. But "right" shouldn't be rigid.

For one thing, costs change from time to time—and sometimes rapidly—as materials or labor get more or less expensive, or as you expand or cut down your overhead. Check your costs regularly and carefully so your cost analysis is accurate and up-to-date. When you're setting price structure, be sure to consider the effect of volume on prices and profits. As you analyze your costs, estimate the savings you might be able to make by increasing volume. Remember, it's always worthwhile to incur an additional dollar of cost as long as you get more than an additional dollar in sales in return.

If you're not certain what your cost complement should be, check with the trade association for your business or profession. They can tell you what's average profit for a business your size. In any case, though, it's important to realize that competition or other circumstances may force you to adjust your net profit up or down, thus changing your cost complement and your prices. You may, for example, want to give a "discount" (earn 10 percent profit rather than a standard 15 percent) to volume customers.

At all times, though, it's essential to know what your full costs are. The markup can be flexible, but the full cost-per-hour figure represents the rock-bottom fee you can get without taking a loss. Keep that in mind, and you'll be in business not just for busy-ness but for profit.

CHAPTER TWELVE

LOW-COST ADVERTISING AND PROMOTION

You don't need a lot of money to help your home business grow. You do, however, need to substitute your lack of dollars with a lot of good sense. Creative thinking and careful planning can be far more valuable to the owner of a growing business than any amount of money. A desirable product or service is not the only requirement for success. There is one essential element that will determine the fate of your business: *marketing*.

Marketing is everything you do to promote your business, from the moment you conceive of it to the point at which customers buy your product or service and begin to patronize your business on a regular basis. It's not possible to succeed without marketing. Advertising and public relations are two major components of marketing, but both can be very costly, and the results are never guaranteed. Large corporations employ advertising agencies and public-relations firms to plan and execute complex advertising and publicity programs at a cost of thousands of dollars per month. Savvy small-business owners learn how to choose the advertising that is just right for their particular business, and develop a favorable public image, using a small amount of capital and their own ingenuity. A carefully planned marketing strategy is reflected in every aspect of your business, from choosing the right name to the color of your packaging. Remember, however, that marketing does not have to be expensive to be effective.

The American Marketing Association calls advertising "any paid communication designed to impart information, develop attitudes, and produce a favorable result for the advertiser." It can be as traditional as a barber pole or as new as the latest in computer graphics. Promotion and advertising can be a heavy expense, especially for a new business that wants to make itself known in the community. A home-based business, however, more often than not has a very limited budget when it comes to advertising. The home business owner needs to make the public aware of his or her product or service at the lowest possible cost.

Most advertising falls into three groups: promoting customer awareness, boosting sales directly, and establishing or changing a business's public image.

A new business has to tell the world that the doors are open. Established businesses need to promote themselves, too, since new customers and competitors are constantly moving into the area. Familiar products are updated; new products and services appear. An aggressive ad policy can help keep your business on the public's mind.

YOUR OWN AD PROGRAM

The first step is to take a hard look at your business, your customers, and your competition. Describe the *ideal* customer as specifically as possible: income, age, number of people in the family, how far they live from your business, shopping habits, and how they see your product or service.

Then develop an *actual* customer profile, an exact description of your best customers: income, age, family size, residence, shopping habits, how they perceive your business. You already have some of the information in order files, charge and credit-card files, and customer lists. You can get more answers by distributing a questionnaire directly to customers. In addition, you can learn a lot just by making note of who buys and the most popular product.

The next step is to look at the competition. What is your share of the market? Who are the main competitors in your trading area? Why would a customer choose a competitor instead of you? What kind of advertising do competitors use? How much does it cost?

The answers point to your own ad program. A restaurant owner who wants high-income diners but advertises low prices is wasting money—advertising the price draws quick, low-budget eaters. If a questionnaire reveals that customers have been passing your store by because they thought your prices were high, ads can change their image of your business.

Other goals might be to: increase store traffic; introduce new products; promote sales, new stores, and special services such as credit plans or delivery; tie in with manufacturers' national promotions; promote specific products. The more specific your advertising goals, the more likely you are to meet them.

HOW MUCH IS ENOUGH?

Advertising is a fixed expense, just like rent and utilities. It's not a luxury to cut back whenever sales slow down. According to the Bank of America in California, businesses that maintain or increase advertising during recessions come out of the slump with a bigger share of the market. The problem is figuring out how much advertising is enough. "All the ads I can afford" is the luxury approach. Matching whatever the competition runs ignores your own needs.

The objective and task method is the most effective way to budget advertising. Set advertising goals, then spend what it costs to buy the ads. Budgeting to meet specific goals will probably have the greatest impact on sales. It's also the most likely to cost more than you can afford.

The percentage of sales method sets a fixed percentage of sales for advertising. Then dollars are allocated to different media. The problem is setting the right percentage. Some large businesses spend .8 to 3 percent of sales on advertising. But what is perfect for one business is too much or too little for another.

Cooperative advertising stretches ad dollars if your home business is affiliated with another company (Tupperware, for example). Co-op ads are an arrangement with a manufacturer or distributor to share the cost of local advertising. Co-ops are almost always restricted to specific brand-name products, but they get your business name connected with nationally recognized products. Co-op arrangements usually cover at least half of the cost of the ad, often including materials such as mats, posters, and radio/TV scripts. You don't have to go it alone preparing ads either. Companies that don't have co-op ad programs may be able to supply ad materials. Most newspaper, radio, and TV outlets can help prepare ads. Some will do almost the whole job for free, others charge a small fee.

Advertising agencies are another possibility, although most are too high-priced for a home business. Agencies advise on what kind of advertising to use, prepare the ads, and place them. In return, the agency collects a commission (usually 15 percent) on the total advertising budget. A small business with a local trading area probably doesn't need—and can't afford—an ad agency on a regular basis. Many agencies, however, accept one-time or project assignments for a flat fee.

Most communities have freelance copywriters who can create newspaper copy, radio jingles, TV scripts, brochures, flyers, or almost any other advertising material. Check the Yellow Pages under "Advertising, Editorial Services," or "Writing Media" sales reps. Other business owners are also good referral sources.

TARGET YOUR MARKET

Having your ads seen by thousands of people isn't enough. They have to be seen by people who might actually buy your product or service. It's called targeting—directing advertising to the people (called markets) most likely to be convinced by your message. A local locksmith should concentrate on local media such as newspapers, shoppers (giveaway papers that are almost all ads), flyers, direct-mail coupons, or posters. A small specialty manufacturer will get better results from trade magazines. TV won't help either one.

The Standard Rate and Data Service (SRDS) can help choose where to run ads. Different SRDS editions cover almost all print and broadcast media. The print-media editions include almost every print publication in the country that accepts advertising, circulations, ad costs, issue dates, and closing dates. Most public libraries and ad agencies have current copies.

Newspapers. Running a newspaper ad has many advantages:

- Ads can be changed quickly.
- They usually never run out of ad space.

- You can specify exactly where ads will run.
- You can even get editorial support—food and housewares in the food and home sections; travel agencies in the travel section.
- Print can convey detailed information, vital if long price and product lists are important.

However, it's also important to remember that almost everybody reads newspapers, making it difficult to target markets, and newspapers may miss younger customers. Another drawback to consider is that the quality of newspaper reproduction is usually low.

Many communities are served by a major daily, local, and weekly paper, as well as shoppers. Locals and weeklies have strong regional identification, an advantage for local advertisers. Shoppers are read by people who are already in a buying mood. All sell space by lines and columns or inches and columns. A 3 × 100-line ad is three columns wide and 100 agate lines deep (14 agate lines per inch), a total of 300 lines. A 3-column × 3″ ad is three columns wide and three inches deep, or nine column inches.

Ad rates are based on circulation. The higher the circulation, the higher the rates. Expect discounts for bulk, frequency, full-page ads, and for advertising in several papers under one ownership. Flat or open rates are nondiscounted rates; a premium is an extra charge for placing an ad in a specific section or page.

Compare prices in Cost Per Thousand (CPM), the cost of reaching 1,000 people with one ad. To compute CPM, divide the cost of the ad by the circulation in thousands. A $500 ad in a 22,000 circulation paper gives a CPM of $22.73 ($500/22). A $600 ad in a 30,000 circulation paper has a CPM of $20. If you're comparing ads of the same size, placement, frequency, and discounts, the lower CPM is usually the better buy.

Magazines. Special-interest magazines (for a specific hobby, geographic area, organization, or activity) and trade magazines (for a specific industry) are an easy way to target your market. Some general-interest publications publish different editions for different groups of readers, another way to target specific markets. The average magazine is read by 4.6 people; each reader sees 85 percent of the ads in each issue. Price is the major disadvantage of magazine ads, though advertising in regional editions can cut the cost in half.

Display ads (anything except classified ads) are sold in fractions of a page: one-sixth, one-fourth, one-third, one-half. Classified ads are sold by the word, line, or by the column inch. Like newspapers, rates increase with the circulation. Prices are compared in CPM.

Radio. There are twice as many radios as people in the U.S., 465 million sets receiving broadcasts from 8,000 stations. Radio also offers lead times as short as a few hours. Because radio stations target their audiences, it's easy to target markets by choosing one station over another.

The disadvantages are that radio spots are too short to cover more than one or two points, and, although ads must be broadcast repeatedly for impact, too much play turns listeners off.

Radio ads are sold in 10-, 30-, and 60-second spots. Rates depend on the length, the time of day, and the size of the listening audience. The most expensive slots are "drive time," 6 to 10 A.M. and 3 to 7 P.M., weekdays. The least expensive slots air between midnight and 5 A.M. Radio stations generally provide CPMs for comparison.

Television. Competition from newspapers and radio has forced TV rates down; co-op ad allowances are up. But businesses that depend on neighborhood trade are probably wasting money on huge TV audiences.

TV time is sold in 15-, 30-, and 60-second spots. Time is purchased in weekly blocks to be aired during specified programs. Cost increases with the size of the viewing audience, expressed in ratings and shares.

One gross rating point (GRP) is one percent of the homes with televisions in the market area. A 12 rating means the show is seen by 12 percent of all TV households. A share is the percentage of TV sets in use that are tuned to a particular show. A program shown at 1 A.M. Monday might have a 2 rating and a 60 share—only 2 percent of all TV homes, but 60 percent of the sets turned on.

Cable TV is usually less expensive than networks and their local affiliates, and it is reaching an ever-growing audience.

Direct mail. Newspapers, magazines, radio, and TV aren't the only media channels that will get your message across. Direct mail, the Yellow Pages, as well as other directories, signs, billboards, and transit ads can be just as effective.

Direct mail may be especially effective for small home-based businesses because (1) it assures you that the consumer will have your whole message, (2) that this is the one who is interested in what you are offering, and (3) your overall cost per prospect is lower. Just as in other forms of advertising, however, you must make sure that your mail piece is appealing and effective. This means hiring a professional graphic artist to prepare your inserts. The cost can be high, but once you have your materials, there will be no further expense until you want to make changes. The look of your printed materials is vitally important, for often your business is judged by the reader's first impression. The copy contained inside your brochure is just as important as the look. If you learn the principles of effective copywriting, you will not have to guess at what to say. If you don't feel you are able to write powerful prose, hire someone who can. It makes no sense to do a mailing that will be deposited in the trash.

Whatever medium you use, use it often. It's easy for a customer to ignore a message seen or heard once, harder the eighth or the tenth time through. Repetition builds business.

MORE IDEAS FOR LOW-COST PROMOTION

There are many other inventive ways to promote your home business. A pet breeder in a large city was struggling with his business for several years—until he came up with a novel idea. He started giving away customized "birth certificates" for the pets he sold. Almost immediately, his sales rose more than 10 percent.

The owner of a new desktop publishing service was trying to attract new clients. She couldn't afford much advertising, so she began offering free "desktop publishing seminars" to civic groups. After two months of seminars, she was swamped with inquiries and clients.

Promotion often makes the crucial difference between business success and failure. Customers or clients must know about a business or a product line before they'll buy, and they must have a reason to buy.

If you are trying to promote your business right now, you can move in one of two directions:

1. You can take the conventional route to promotion and mount an elaborate media campaign, spending a considerable amount of money.
2. You can let your creative juices flow and mount a low-cost

promotion effort, using a potpourri of attention-getting gim-
micks to bring your message to the buying public.

Now, to be sure, conventional advertising is valuable. If your enterprise is large enough, or if you're selling numerous product lines, you
may find that a full-fledged media campaign is the most efficient and
cost-effective way to promote your business. If money is tight, however, or you're not sure you can amortize the heavy costs of a media
campaign over a period of time, here is an assortment of low-cost
promotional techniques you can try. Not all may be appropriate for your
particular business, and certainly it would be costly to try all of them.
But you're sure to find some ideas that will work for you and your
particular home business.

Giveaways. People love to receive "free" items, especially things
they can use to gain knowledge or improve their lives. You can base an
entire promotional campaign on this desire. If you're running a
furniture-repair business, for instance, you could give away a furniture-
repair brochure, free furniture-planning guides, or color swatches.
Once you begin giving away authoritative information, customers will
begin to perceive you as an expert in your field.

News Creation. Want to put names and news from your business
into the local newspapers? It may be easier than you think. If you don't
have any news to report to the local media, create some. Maybe you've
taken on a new associate. Or maybe you're selling an unusual product
line. Or maybe you've opened a free advice center for the community.
Or maybe you've received an award from a civic or professional group.
Local *PennySaver*s and weeklies are often quite interested in business
news of this sort and can help you attract the attention of thousands of
people.

Events. You may be able to attract the attention of the media or a
crowd by staging a special promotional event. If you run fitness classes,
for instance, you could stage a celebrity instructor day (perhaps a
popular local radio DJ). If you're promoting a new real-estate business,
you can offer tours of a model home in the area. If you're selling
children's products and it's springtime, you can offer lunch with the
Easter bunny. Get the idea?

Charity Tie-ins. Are you launching a new product? Trying to increase visibility among a particular segment of your community? Offer

your product to one or more local charities as a raffle prize or for use at a fund-raising event. You'll receive lots of exposure among people who buy tickets or attend the event.

Contests. Offer a desirable or unique item—or even several items—as contest prizes. First, find a contest theme that ties into your business. A caterer might offer a quiche-eating contest. A photographer might offer a young model contest. A mail-order craft firm might offer an "Early American" handicrafts contest. Invite contest submissions and offer prizes to the winners. Do contests attract attention? You bet. All it takes is a few signs, a small press announcement or two, and the word will spread throughout the community grapevine.

Community Service. Nothing brings you to the attention of people faster—or more favorably—than community service. Ask yourself how your enterprise can be a "good neighbor" to your community. If you're running a lawn care and gardening service, perhaps you can offer one season's services at no charge to a needy charitable organization or nursing home in your area. Hundreds of people will hear about your work in the process. Volunteer for various community causes. If appropriate, you can step in during a community emergency, offering products and services to help an organization or individuals in need.

Couponing. Americans are very coupon-conscious. Test the market: at what level will coupons increase the volume of various product or service lines? When you get some tentative answers, start distributing coupons that offer a discount on your services. Distribute them in area newspapers, on store counters, in door-to-door mail packets (which can often be quite inexpensive), at the public library, at laundromats, at any location where people congregate.

Badges and Novelties. You can easily and inexpensively produce badges, bumper stickers, book covers, and other novelty items for distribution in your area. You can imprint your business name and the first names of customers on many of these products at little cost and distribute them for free. Or you can tie your novelty program into a contest: once a month, you can offer a prize to anyone you encounter who happens to be sporting one of your badges, or to anyone whose car happens to carry one of your bumper stickers. Or you can distribute bumper stickers or badges with peel-off coupons, redeemable at your place of business.

Celebrity Visits. With a bit of persistence you may be able to arrange to have a local media celebrity, public official, or entertainment personality—even a fictitious cartoon character or clown—visit your service. The celebrity can sign autographs, read stories to children, perform a cooking demonstration, or perform any one of a hundred other traffic-building activities.

Celebrate Holidays. You'll probably want to celebrate major public holidays with special sales. But celebrate some of the offbeat holidays as well. Almost every business has a few little-known holidays. Ever hear of National Pickle Day, for instance? Or Cat Lovers Month? Once you find the "right" holiday, you can sponsor a special sale or special product offer or arrange special media coverage of a holiday event.

Go Where the People Are. Can you open sales or information booths at community fairs and festivals? This promotional technique can work wonders for gift retailers, craftspeople, and personal service firms. If you have the people and the time, can you handle regional fairs or even trade shows?

Mailing Lists. Once you begin establishing a committed clientele, gather their names on a mailing list. Save the names from your mail orders and telephone inquiries. Eventually you'll be able to send product circulars or even catalogs to the folks on your list and you'll be able to promote your products by mail.

Scavenger Hunts. If you want people to buy *now*, offer them an unbeatable deal. If they bring an old product—a small appliance, a book, whatever—to you, you'll give them a worthwhile discount on a comparable new item. Or stage a general-purpose scavenger hunt. Customers who bring in three items of canned goods for your community's food bank will receive a discount on products purchased that day.

Parties. Everyone loves a party. Why not celebrate the anniversary of your business or some special holiday by offering baked goods and beverages? If you're running a service business, perhaps you can offer an open house or obtain a small banquet room in your community. Besides refreshments, be sure the place is brightly decorated. And you might even want to offer simple gifts.

Greeting Cards. Do you send out greeting cards to major customers or clients? Holidays, birthdays, and anniversaries make nice greeting-card occasions. Greeting cards create enormous goodwill and keep your name in front of people.

Seminars. In this information-hungry age, people love to receive advice, especially about their personal needs and hobbies. If you sell health foods or run fitness classes, perhaps you can offer "wellness" seminars during lunchtime to your area's business community. If you're an interior decorator, perhaps you can offer one-hour decorating workshops to any group of ten persons who will gather in someone's home.

If you're not pleased with your promotional efforts today, or if you simply must increase your exposure among customers and prospects—it's probably time to increase your publicity efforts. By all means advertise in the media if you can or must. But don't neglect your greatest promotional asset—your mind. Ponder the products, services, and events you can offer the community and devise a creative promotional strategy around them. You'll have to invest a bit of time and energy in the project, but the payoff will be worth it. You'll save hundreds—or even thousands—of advertising dollars and, better yet, you'll travel a well-worn shortcut to profit.

CHAPTER THIRTEEN

BEATING THE COMPETITION

"If only I had no competition, I could make a fortune." You may have heard that from other small-business owners, or you may have even said it yourself. But the reality is, most likely, that you do have competition. And if you don't have any competition, and your product or service is a good one, you soon will. Not that competition is all bad. In fact, it can even help your business. First, it's easier to get a decision from a customer when he has a choice between product A and product B rather than between product A and nothing. Second, as every athlete knows, participating in a game is a much better muscle-builder than calisthenics. Your business can actually become better because of the competition.

Your competition *can* help you, providing you know how to use it. Here are ten ways to put your competition to work for you—and thereby beat them at the game of business!

1. MASTER YOUR FIELD

No matter how much you think you know about your product, it's likely that you don't know *everything*. Usually, a home business has a particular specialty, an area in which it outshines its rivals. Your company may be first in quality, but your competition may have a better ad campaign. You may be ahead when it comes to service, but perhaps your competitor beats you in price. Whatever your competitor's strong point is, find out all you can about it. The result will be an addition to the sum total of your knowledge—knowledge that helps you grow.

How can you find out about the competition? Just become a customer and examine his product. Study his advertisements. Send for any literature which he might offer.

2. PINPOINT HIS WEAKNESSES

Once you know where your competitor is vulnerable, you can concentrate on the superior features that you have to offer. A thorough and critical examination of his literature, his products and services can be revealing.

If you know your competitor's customers, talk with them. They might tell you about defects in and dissatisfactions with what your competitor sells or makes. Get those vulnerable points down on paper, then write your corresponding strong points beside them. If you don't have strong points in those areas, implement them; play these "trump cards" in your advertising.

3. PINPOINT YOUR WEAKNESSES

Careful study of your competitor's product and methods can help you determine your own soft spots—those points at which *you* are vulnerable. When you know what they are, you can seek out ways to compensate for them. If they are subject to improvement—for example, poor service—you can take the extra time and effort necessary to rectify them. If they are not subject to improvement—for instance, your competitor sells a product with a patented feature that you cannot duplicate—you can study your product and find a feature that cancels his advantage, one that you can put forth as a greater value.

4. ANTICIPATE OBJECTIONS

Find out what customers might find objectionable about your product or service. Even if they won't tell you directly, you might get a good line on their objections by paying close attention to the types of questions they ask you. Also, if you know customers of your competitor, ask them why they haven't tried your product. Make a list of all objectionable claims and write down opposite them the facts to refute them.

5. USE COMPETITION AS A SELLING LEVER

If you know a potential customer is seriously considering patronizing your competition, don't interpret that as your cue to give up. Rather, take it for what it is: a legitimate buying signal. The customer is interested in buying your type of product; your competition has done half of your work for you. All that remains for *you* to get the sale is to convince the customer that your product or service is superior.

6. DETERMINE YOUR CUSTOMER'S "HOT BUTTONS"

Frequently, a customer fails to buy because a business neglects to mention the one consideration that weighs heavily with her or him. It isn't always easy to figure out what that factor is, but there are various clues to look for. One of the best clues is what your prospect says about your competition.

Often, a prospect will drop references to your competitor that are almost as good as a blueprint of his particular desires. For example, if the prospect mentions that Competitor A offers a similar product for less money, then you know that this prospect's hot button is money. That is your cue to either come down in price, if you can, or point out how your product will save him more money in the long run.

7. INCREASE ENTHUSIASM AND SELF-ESTEEM

Whenever you find your enthusiasm waning for your own product line, visit the competitor. Make a critical comparison between products. By the time you leave, you may be enthusiastically resold on your product. This enthusiasm will carry over to your advertising and, ultimately, your customers.

8. CLOSE SALES

Frequently, a prospect is undecided between your product and that of a competitor. Your job, then, is to tip the scale in your favor. One man who owns a home-based advertising service devised this approach: He hands his prospect a pen, lays a sheet of paper in front of him or her, and says, "Here's a list of what you'll get from our service. Would you mind checking off the things you will be getting from the other source you are considering?"

Aside from learning a lot about his competition through this technique, this man subtly forces his prospect to make his own comparison between the two services under consideration.

9. LEARN FROM YOUR COMPETITOR'S MISTAKES

Every business person should learn from his or her mistakes, but you can also learn from the mistakes your competitor makes.

Roger L. runs a lawn-care service and received a call from a company with about three acres of grass. This company had been using one of Roger's competitors, but became dissatisfied with his service. The company complained to Roger that the competitor didn't come every week, as contracted, and neglected to trim around all sidewalks—in other words, they did a slipshod job. Not only did Roger win the contract from this company, but he also became more diligent about serving his other customers, learning that a less than excellent job could lose clients. Roger's competitor helped Roger's business a great deal.

10. BORROW IDEAS

If it is true that you can learn from a competitor's mistakes, it is equally true that you can cash in on a rival's successes. This doesn't mean you should be blindly imitative. It does mean that you ought to be alert to ideas that can stimulate your own thinking. How, precisely, can you adapt Competitor A's successful use of direct mail? What can you learn from Competitor B's computerization? What is the logical extension of

Competitor C's use of customer surveys? Questions like these will stir your own creative juices, and some of the answers will amaze you. Here are some other important questions you should find answers to:

- What services are offered by competitors that you don't offer?
- Are you and your employees (if any) as well qualified to serve as specialists or customer problem-solvers as your competitor?
- Do your competitors accept credit cards or charge cards for their services that you don't accept?
- How does your company image compare to your competitors'?
- Can you answer questions about your competitor's products and services knowledgeably and objectively?
- Who keeps more complete records on each customer, you or your competitor?
- Do you mail a thank-you letter after each sales call, whether or not a sale was made? Does your competitor?
- What equipment does your competitor use that is better than yours?
- How many times has your competitor had his name in newspapers in the past three months? Count only the times for free publicity such as announcements, promotions, seminars, sponsorships, donations, speeches, etc. How many times has your name been published for these reasons?
- How much advertising (number and size/time) does your competitor do each month? How much do you do?

A new look at your competition as described here will prove what some business people have always known: competition, properly harnessed, can work *for*—not against—you.

CHAPTER FOURTEEN

BUILDING REPEAT CUSTOMERS

Every home business owner should know how to reap rewards from his or her list of present and prospective customers. By understanding some basic principles and following some general procedures, you can take advantage of the kind of marketing power that has made millions of dollars for direct-mail marketers across the country.

Whether you have ten or 10,000 customers, your mailing list is a valuable commodity. If you're not making the best use of your customer and prospect names, you could be losing hundreds—even thousands— of dollars each year! Let's take a look at a few examples that demonstrate why your list is so valuable.

Let's say you own a small ceramics business in your home and have decided to introduce an advanced ceramics class. You've placed an ad in the local paper. However, if you've maintained a list of people who have already taken your beginning class, you could send them a letter telling them about the advanced class.

If you charge $20 for the class and you have 100 previous students, your mailing cost would be approximately $30 (postage and printing). You only need two previous students to sign up for the new class to make your promotional effort pay off. Chances are you'll get at least a 5-percent response; that's five students. And, depending on how much the students liked your first class and how often they buy from you, your response can be substantially higher. If you haven't kept track of those names, however, you'll simply have to rely on the newspaper ad to get new students.

As another example, let's say you own a small mail-order business which sells specialty items. You have recently introduced some new items that are similar to some of your bestsellers. If you've kept track of the people who purchased from you before, you can now tell them about the new products you have. Chances are they'll be very good prospects.

Are you making the best use of your customer file? Do you:

- Know who your past customers are?
- Make use of follow-up sales promotions?
- Keep an active prospect list?
- Have a means of identifying recent purchasers and purchasers of specific products?

TWO TYPES OF IN-HOUSE LISTS AND HOW TO MAINTAIN THEM

As a business owner or manager, you should be cultivating two types of lists: a customer list and a prospect list. Each list is a valuable commodity to you, and each list should be maintained in a slightly different way.

Customer List

Your customer list is a list of those people who have bought goods or services from you in the past. When you speak of a customer, you are speaking of a person who has paid for your goods and services. Maintenance of your customer list involves adding customer names, updating addresses, and adding other information. You must also delete names of people who have not been customers for a while.

One of the big questions you will need to ask yourself as you begin to build a customer "database" is, "What information do I want to keep on each customer?" The answer depends on both your marketing approach and on the capability of your computer system. (If you don't own a computer, the answer to this question will depend on how much time you or one of your employees has to devote to manually maintaining a list.)

Generally, the following information is considered standard: full name, address, phone number, and purchase history (including both an itemization of what they have bought from you in the past and the date of their last purchase).

You will probably find it more useful to access this information based on what and when they last purchased. For instance, in the first example above, you would want to be able to generate a list of all those people who attended your beginning ceramics class. In the second example, you would want to be able to generate a list of those people who bought items.

You'll need to think of all the ways you'll want to be able to access and sort information before you set up your database.

Prospect List

Your prospect list is a list of those people who, for some reason, you feel may someday become customers. You may feel this way because they've expressed an interest in your products or services, because they were referred to you by a current customer, or because you know they have interests that indicate they might be potential customers.

The type of information you will want to keep on prospects includes: full name, address, phone number, how or why they were added to your list.

Suppose the ad you placed for your advanced ceramics class generated several responses. You coded this ad "C2" and entered the name, address, and phone number of each person that called in response to the ad. Later you decide to do a mailing offering these people a special discount on the class if they sign up by a certain date. You would certainly want the ability to retrieve those names from your computer (or manual system). Since you've used a special code (C2), you'll easily be able to do this.

What happens when a prospect becomes a customer? Simply add this name to your customer list and remove it from your prospect list. If your computer isn't advanced enough to accept a program that will make this transfer automatically, you may need to go through each list on a regular basis (perhaps quarterly) to update both files. This would involve checking each name on the prospect list to see if it shows up on the customer list as well. If it does, delete it from the prospect list.

This procedure helps you assure accuracy in your mailings. It also gives you some indication of how successful you have been at turning prospects into customers.

TEN TIPS FOR GETTING THE MOST FROM YOUR MAILING LISTS

The mailing list is a powerful marketing tool. Learning to use your lists to their best advantage can be a constant and challenging task. The following ten tips can get you off to a good start.

1. Acquire names whenever and wherever you can. Names mean money. Every time you can add a name to your list, whether it's a customer name or a prospect name, you're adding the potential for a future sale. There are numerous ways to generate the names you'll need and make sure that you "capture" them. This is where your creativity will come into play.

2. If you offer classes or seminars as a way of increasing business, make sure you enter your entire student roster (both those students who completed the entire course and those who signed up but never "showed"). Place the latter on your prospect list.

3. Whenever you make a sale, ask for the customer's name, address, and phone number. Make this a part of your procedure for issuing a sales receipt. If the customer writes a check, except for the phone number, you can get the information you need directly from that check.

4. Post flyers with tear-off forms on community bulletin boards (such as in grocery stores) which say, for example, "We're constantly adding new products and offering new courses. Would you like to be on our mailing list? Please fill out one of the forms beside this box." Add these names to your prospect list. This is a good way of capturing the names of people who just *might* be interested but haven't yet purchased anything.

5. When you place ads in the paper, always include a coupon or response device of some sort that requires a name, address, and phone number. The response may simply be "for more information." This not only helps you build your prospect list, it also helps you track the responsiveness of your space advertisements.

6. Stage an event at a local store or mall. Perhaps you could arrange

a demonstration of a ceramics class. As part of the event include a drawing where the prize is a free class or a free product from your store. Add every name, address, and phone number you receive for the drawing to your prospect list.

7. Ask for referrals. Offer special "gifts" to customers who can "get a friend to . . ." You now have a new customer to add to your list.

8. Mail to your customers regularly. "Your best customers are your best customers." This may seem like a silly statement, but it's true. You need to keep your customers loyal. One way of doing this is by constantly reminding them that you're still around. Develop a newsletter that you can mail regularly to your customer list, or send letters regularly which tell about upcoming sales, classes, etc.

9. Take advantage of every opportunity to promote new products and services to customers who have made similar purchases in the past. This type of promotion is one of the most effective for any direct marketer.

10. Keep your list "clean." Old names do nothing more than take up space. If customers haven't responded for quite some time, jostle their memory and ask them if they want to stay on your mailing list. You should schedule a regular (perhaps semiannual) mailing to customers who haven't been "active" for months. In the mailing you could say: "We want you back! If we don't hear from you by (give a date), we'll be forced to remove your name from our mailing list." Include a promotion for a new product with the mailing to help defray some of the costs. Remove the names of nonrespondents and update the history of those who do respond.

Savvy advertisers know the value of their in-house mailing list. By setting up a good system for your customer and prospect names and taking advantage of the ten tips above, you too can benefit from some of these secrets.

CHAPTER FIFTEEN

BUDGETING AND RECORD-KEEPING; BILLING AND COLLECTIONS

A well-organized record-keeping system is at the heart of any successful home business, since it helps you to see that expenses do not outrun revenues. Records are also needed to satisfy creditors, bankers, vendors, customers, and tax authorities and various other agencies. Depending on the way records are kept, they can be either a millstone—a near useless collection of paper—or a lifeline and guide to productivity and profit.

An accountant should be consulted to establish a record system very early in the life of your business. Don't call him or her at the end of the fiscal year when chaos reigns, but invite him at the start, so he can instruct you or your bookkeeper in the proper forms and entries. Here, too, is where a computer can be helpful. Accounting and general-ledger software is available to help make this entire task easy for you. The software has built-in forms (or you can usually create your own) and the accompanying manual instructs about proper entry. The software may not be able to take the place of a good accountant, but it can ease your day-to-day use of an accounting system.

You may see your business in terms of a concrete product or service, but your accountant sees it as paper or data: journals, ledgers, checkbooks, receipts, cash disbursements, payrolls, and income statements (some software can handle all of these tasks). It is wise to be guided by this system of record-keeping, for it will give you an early warning when things are going wrong. It will tell you when additional money is needed and whether or not your business is profitable.

Small businesses must cope with seven categories of records, even though some overlap, and, depending on the size and nature of your business, some may not apply at all.

1. **Company records.** Bylaws, partnership papers, incorporation papers, copyrights, patents, contracts, labor agreements, cashbooks, checks, pension papers, tax returns, deeds, and leases.
2. **Accounting records.** Journals, ledgers, audit reports, payroll checks and records, time sheets, vouchers to employees and vendors, trial balance sheets, bank statements, and dividend checks.
3. **Correspondence.** General and legal letters, correspondence dealing with purchases, licensing, and production.
4. **Purchases and sales.** Invoices, contracts, requisitions, and purchase orders.
5. **Traffic.** Shipping, freight bills, bills of lading manifests, export declarations.
6. **Insurance.** Policies, claims, and premium notices.
7. **Personnel.** Employment records, disability and sick pay claims and benefits, recommendations, and withholding statements.

Generally, records should be kept six years before they are destroyed. Some records obviously must be kept for the life of your business and should never (or at least not until six years after it closes its doors) be destroyed.

Which records you will maintain will depend on your needs, how you use your information, how you use your accountant's advice, and the record-keeping system you establish. Very soon after starting up, if not earlier, you must choose between a cash or accrual method of accounting. In the cash method, revenue is considered earned only upon actual receipt of payment; expenses are considered only when actually paid. In the accrual method, revenue is considered earned when the goods have been sold or the service performed; actual payment may not be received for some time. On the other hand, costs are shown as incurred when purchases have been executed, even though no payment is made.

Simple home businesses may wish to use the cash method, for it may require no more than a checking account and billing system. A consultant or service business, a business which has few sales (though presumably large ones), may well find the cash method sufficient for its needs. However, the cash method does not reflect the true status of the business at any given moment—it neglects accounts payable and accounts receivable.

The accrual method is more complicated, but since it considers spending and receiving immediately, the owner knows exactly where he or she stands at any point. Some businesses are required by law to adopt accrual accounting, especially where significant inventories enter into the picture, but most entrepreneurs can make a choice to suit their needs.

The next choice a home business operator must face is whether to have single-entry or double-entry bookkeeping. For simple businesses, single-entry records may be perfectly adequate—every transaction is handled separately, with incoming and outgoing monies entered into the check register or account book, and the separation of bills and receipts.

Double-entry bookkeeping is a way of double-checking things, since it is based on one idea: all transactions consist of an exchange of one thing for another. Thus, every entry of a credit must have its counterpart in a debit entry. When money is spent, cash on hand is reduced, but on the other side, some expense has been reduced or some asset of value has been acquired. This balancing provides a cross-check on what is actually happening to the cash flow.

To keep a double-entry system, you will need either the proper software program (many make double entries automatically) or a journal and ledger. All transactions are first entered into the journal, and then are summarized on a monthly basis in the appropriate column in the ledger (again, many computer programs perform this posting automatically). A ledger has five categories of information: income, expense, asset, liability, and net worth.

Entries in the income-and-expense columns are crossed out yearly. The other categories of asset, liability, and net worth are kept on a continuing basis; these will show the condition or financial position of the business as of a given date. These three categories are the essentials of your balance sheet.

DO IT THE EASY WAY

Here are several hints that will ease your record-keeping load.

Number your forms sequentially. Statements, bills, invoices, purchase orders, petty cash vouchers, and checks all need an identifying number. If you want to see how your business shapes up before spending money on stationery printed to order, use pre-printed forms and hand-number them. You can always switch to a more sophisticated or computerized system later, but the conversion will be much easier when each transaction has its own identifying number.

Copy your transactions. Whether you use carbon paper, carbonless copy paper, or photocopying, you should have at least one record of your transactions and as many duplicates as you may need. You may want a copy to file by number, by customer's last name, by date, by source, or by item. Try to plan the minimum number of copies you'll need, but be flexible. You may find after several months you rarely use one set of files but could use a more convenient set. Having the duplicates available lets you reshuffle your files to fit your changing needs.

If you can afford a computer-accounting or database system, it will make all of this sorting and numbering much easier. Once records are entered, they can then be sorted by any category you choose. Just be sure to make backups of all computer data.

Date your transactions. Even-numbering and duplicating a date may be the last and sometimes best resort for tracing an order. It's one more cross-reference at your disposal.

File your forms. Whether you use a nail on a piece of wood, a shoebox, file cards, a file cabinet, or a computer database, file your forms and correspondence so they can be easily retrieved. We don't recommend a shoebox, and you may not need a computer, but you must have a system that is compatible with your operation.

Keep calendars. A calendar that shows when goods and supplies will probably have to be reordered and when bills are due can help you anticipate your obligations. Another useful record to keep, especially if you don't salary yourself, is a time calendar that indicates how many hours you spent working on your business.

BILLING

Most home business owners don't need to bill their customers. Because the majority of home businesses are personal services of one kind or another, the home business operator expects payment from the client upon completion of the work. Pet-sitting, appliance repair, frame making, firewood delivery—all of these types of businesses can ask the customer to pay the bill on the spot.

Your customers will pay with personal checks or cash, and you may be tempted to stuff the cash into your pocket and use it to pick up items at the grocery store. Don't do it. Even though this form of billing and payment is quite informal, you must treat it in a formal and business-like manner. All cash and check payments should be recorded and deposited as soon as possible into your business account. If you don't keep formal records of all your income—especially the cash—you may never know how successful your business is. And it should go without saying that these records are necessary for income tax purposes (see Chapter 17).

Many home businesses will bill their customers in a more formal manner. If you run a consulting business, for example, or you perform services such as word processing for other businesses, these clients will expect to be billed. The time frame for such billing should be worked out when your services are contracted, but generally you send your bills out at the end of the month with the stipulation that they be paid within thirty days.

To bill your customers, it is important that you have kept strict records of the amount and type of work you have performed or, if you're working on a price-per-hour basis, exactly how many hours you worked. You should have an invoice number for each bill that you send out to help keep track of what has and has not been paid. Ready-made invoice forms can be purchased at some stationery stores, business-supply stores, and mail-order houses.

What do you do if the customer does not pay within the requested thirty days? That comes under the heading of collections.

COLLECTIONS

If yours is not an all-cash business, it is inevitable that you are going to
have some problems collecting on overdue bills from a small percentage of your customers. A collection system is necessary, but it need
not—and probably should not—be impersonal. At times you have to
guess who among your collection-problem customers are unwilling but
able to pay, and who are both unwilling and unable.

Your collection procedure should be deliberately planned so that it
will move in a regular and orderly way through a series of steps, the
collection effort gradually becoming more and more insistent until final
decisive action is taken. The procedure should be organized into the
following four logical steps:

1. Reminding the customer
2. Requesting response
3. Insisting on payment
4. Final action

Reminding the Customer

All those customers who do not respond to your invoice or statement
within the time limit set by you must be reminded that their accounts
have become past-due. The tone of the first reminder should be mild,
because the only reasonable assumption you can make at this point is
that the customer has simply overlooked the matter.

Good methods for giving the past-due customer a reminder are:
printed or photocopied form notices in the shape of a card or slip of
paper about 3" × 5"; duplicate or short-form statements with or without
a reminder message in the form of a sticker, insert, or written, typed, or
rubber-stamped appeals; telephone calls. In most lines of business,
collection letters and personal calls are best reserved for later steps in a
company's collection procedure.

Whether you wish to improve collections by reminding past-due
accounts promptly is a matter that is up to you. But normally you don't
have to worry about incurring ill-will by promptness in reminding,
provided the content of the first notice is not offensive. Its impersonal
form should indicate that the customer is not being singled out for

discriminatory action, but is receiving the same treatment accorded all others.

Requesting Response

Customers who do not react to the simple reminder should be automatically subjected to the second step of collection follow-up after a predetermined number of days. The message used should not only remind the customer of her or his debt, but also should ask for a response.

The tone should still be mild and courteous, but the purpose of the second step is to find out why the customer is slow in paying and what can be done to remedy the difficulty. Impersonal notices on paper or 3″ × 5″ cards are effective. So are telephone calls and short form-letters.

Insisting on Payment

Customers who have not responded by now require a third step in which a still different procedure is applied. It has been some time now since you notified the customer by sending him an invoice or statement. Later, you reminded him of his failure to pay as agreed. Then you reminded him again with a request for some kind of response. You still have not been able to get in touch with him, and he has not contacted you.

As you prepare to take the third step, it is reasonable for you to begin to suspect that the customer may prove to be unwilling, and perhaps does not intend to pay his bill at all. You are therefore now justified in bearing down and applying increasing pressure.

The content of the third-step collection messages may include various pressures: temporary suspension of credit privileges on the past-due account; threats to report the account to the credit bureau, the firm's legal department, a collection agency, or an attorney; and, in the case of installment sales, threats to repossess or sue.

In lines other than installment buying, it is difficult to justify permitting more than fifteen days to elapse between an unanswered request for response and the beginning of the stage where you insist on payment.

Final Action

In analyzing the customers who have failed to pay or make satisfactory arrangements to liquidate their indebtedness to you after the preceding three steps in collection follow-up, you will find that they fall into two main classes:

1. Those who are able to pay and must be forced to do so. If these people owe you enough money, they should be traced and suits should be brought if the amount they owe merits the expense of collecting.
2. Those who are willing but cannot pay in full, or who cannot pay within a reasonable amount of time. You may be able to induce these customers to reevaluate their financial position and find some way to pay within a reasonable period.

The trick with collections, especially for a home-based business that is small, is not to spend more money collecting than you are owed. If you go about your collection problems—and chances are there won't be many—along the lines I have suggested, you will collect from most overdue accounts by yourself, without outside help.

CHAPTER SIXTEEN

HIRING YOUR FIRST EMPLOYEE

When you get to the point where you're making money but are always feeling rushed, harried, and bogged down by paperwork, it may be time to hire a part-time employee for your home business. Getting help will free you from many office details and get you back to where you belong: promoting your product or service and taking time to be with your family.

Many home business operators prefer to keep it all in the family and hire a son, daughter, niece, or nephew to work a few hours a week. If you must go to the outside, however, and hire a stranger, following these guidelines will make finding good help much easier.

CHECK THE LAWS

No matter how many people you hire, full- or part-time, you'll be responsible for taxes, forms, and insurance requirements. All the federal forms and taxes will apply to you and, depending on what city and state you're in, you will also be responsible for state and possibly city taxes and forms.

Contact your local government agencies and get information about your responsibilities before you hire an employee. Ask them to send you the necessary forms, timetables for filing, etc., so you will be prepared.

If you don't understand exactly what your responsibilities are after reading their literature, call the agency and ask. There are penalties and fees for late filing of these taxes and forms, and it's illegal not to pay them at all.

DEFINE THE JOB

Your first step will be to determine what kind of help you need. For many, that first employee is usually a "girl or man Friday"—someone to help with general office duties. List the necessary duties. They might include, for example, record-keeping, handling mail, filing, answering the telephone, processing orders, and typing.

Keeping records may also require keeping track of inventory and maintaining a simple set of books. A great deal of time will probably be spent typing routine items such as labels, addresses, invoice reports, and correspondence. Miscellaneous duties might include opening and sorting of mail, stuffing envelopes, delivering messages, and other routine office tasks.

Define the job to yourself. What qualifications are needed? What are the exact duties? Is experience necessary? What can you afford to pay? If you know the answers to these questions you will be more apt to attract applicants who are interested in that kind of work. Salary will depend on how much experience you desire as well as the amount of work and the skills needed. Pay will range from minimum wage and up, depending on your geographical area and the size and nature of your business.

Many office workers are covered by life insurance and health and accident insurance (paid all or in part by you) and also have paid sick leaves. Although you may not offer all of these benefits, remember that those competing for the same help probably will.

Motivation is as important as skill. You not only want to get a good employee, but to have one who is satisfied and will be with you for a long time.

LET THE WORD OUT

To get the maximum number of applicants, you might want to advertise in local papers. A good ad will specify the nature of the work, duties, salary, and whether or not experience is required. If you are flexible on salary, you could say "depends on experience." Be sure the ad clearly defines the position. It's cheaper in the long run to spend more on an ad that will eliminate the unqualified than to waste your time interviewing applicants who don't meet your requirements.

PROPER SCREENING

Now you need to prepare yourself for the responses. Get some application forms, often sold in stationery stores, to help you weed out the people you don't want to interview. An application won't necessarily tell you if someone will fill the job, but it can often tell you if he or she can't. You will be able to see at a glance if the applicant meets your requirements. After you receive the application, scan it and determine if an interview is necessary.

THE INTERVIEW

As you probably remember from your own job-hunting experiences, an interview can be enjoyable or uncomfortable. Now the tables are turned and it will be you who will set the stage. Begin by putting the applicant at ease. This can be in the form of an invitation to sit down or in comments about the weather. After your first, interviews will come naturally.

An interview is a means of establishing personal, subjective contact with the person or persons who might be working with you. Prospective employees want to find out about hours, pay, the working environment, duties, and how you seem to come across as a possible boss.

Ten minutes can generally tell you if the person will not do, but you will want to put in more time if you think he or she might be the right applicant. So get the applicant talking. Try asking about education and work experience. Remember that good talkers aren't necessarily good doers. Some people can sound intelligent without being so.

No amount of time, trouble, and effort spent in selection is ever wasted if it helps you make the right choice. It's mainly a matter of elimination. You don't want someone who isn't able to get the work done, but it's just as important not to "overhire." A bored employee soon leaves.

MAKING THE RIGHT DECISION

The best workers are not only self-motivated, but well trained and supervised. Even someone who has done this type of work before must be trained in your methods. Be sure to check out the application. Call references and past employers. Check the person's past position, responsibilities, salary, and reason for leaving.

One of the most important things to consider is personal rapport. Do you feel comfortable with this person? Is the applicant alert, responsible, trustworthy, intelligent, and able to work alone if your own work takes you away from your home office? You don't want to invite tensions, so get someone you like and can work with easily.

TRAINING FOR THE FUTURE

Don't let a new employee fend for herself or himself. Impressions obtained in the first day or week are lasting. Set up specific on-the-job training procedures. Let your employee know that after a probationary period you will review overall performance. Discharge the person if you have doubts about job ability: Keeping an unsuitable person does both the employee and yourself a disservice. Giving a wage increase at the end of the probationary period is a positive way of showing the new employee that you appreciate good efforts.

Explain the day-to-day running of the business. Take a few minutes a few times a week to explain how the employee's work fits into the general activity of your home business. Once routines are established and operating smoothly, delegate interesting but time-consuming tasks that you would otherwise have to do yourself. Do all you can to encourage your first assistant.

CHAPTER SEVENTEEN

TAXES—WHAT'S DEDUCTIBLE

The Internal Revenue Service (IRS) doesn't define your activities exactly the same way you do. For example, if you start a home-based business and don't show a profit in any two of a five-year period, the IRS will consider your occupation strictly as a "hobby" and not a "business."

"In that case," says IRS spokesman Steve Pyrek, "deductions and business expenses are disallowable."

If you qualify as a business, however, various kinds of advantages are offered to you by the IRS. You may, for example, deduct a percentage of your rent or mortgage if you work out of your home. Utility bills are also allowable deductions, but "within reason." In other words, all deductions of utilities and home use must be based on the percentage of space you use in your home or apartment that is devoted exclusively to your business. You can't deduct the entire rent bill of a three-bedroom house, for example, if you're using only one of the bedrooms for your business.

Other allowable deductions include:

- Costs for equipment repairs
- Rental costs, as long as the rental was used for conducting business
- Expenses incurred in entertaining guests, prospects, and clients

- Costs related to the purchase of educational, informational, and professional literature that would in some way improve your skills
- Expenses incurred for labor, such as a secretary or bookkeeper
- Insurance costs for equipment, automobile, and/or other owned vehicle

Your business equipment, a computer, typewriter, and office furniture are capital assets that can be deducted either in their entirety on the first year of purchase, or over five years, depending on your bookkeeping methods. Consult your accountant, the IRS, or a tax-preparation service such as H&R Block for more complete information.

DON'T FIGHT IT

Do you think the Internal Revenue Service doesn't know or care about your home business? Think again. They may not, but is it worth the risk? Hiding your business activities from the IRS probably won't save you money, and it could be a costly mistake.

If your business is still young and struggling, your fear of filing is understandable. You think that it doesn't make sense to report a business that isn't generating much income. You don't want to be bothered with all of the paperwork, and you can't afford to pay more taxes. These are common misconceptions. There is no way that you can advertise, publicize, or market a business that is being hidden. In most cases there is only one form used to report income or loss from a business or profession. And neglecting to report your legitimate expenses (which can be especially high during the start-up phase of your business) can cost you valuable tax deductions.

You should seek out professional help when it is time to prepare your taxes. To find the right person to help you, ask other home business owners for a recommendation. Use someone who is familiar with the particular laws that affect your type of business. But keep in mind that hiring an accountant does not relieve you of your basic responsibilities. Make sure that you have a basic understanding of tax laws and procedures. That way, you will be able to give your accountant more valuable input when it is time to file your return.

To qualify for all those valuable deductions that come with business ownership, it is important to erase any doubt that your business will be classified as a hobby. If your business generates a profit in three out of five consecutive years, it should be considered a business. But there are other criteria that can be used to prove that your enterprise is indeed being operated with the intent to make a profit.

Make sure that you register your business in accordance with your state's requirements as outlined in previous chapters. Keep accounting records (a detailed checkbook register may be sufficient during your first year) and develop an advertising and marketing plan that will demonstrate how you expect to make a profit in the future. Save copies of any advertisements, press releases, and other marketing activities to show your past attempts to increase business. If your home business is a moonlighting activity, and you have substantial income from another job, you will have to take special care to prove that you are attempting to develop a money-making enterprise.

Once you decide to take the legal road for your home business, you will be able to take advantage of many legal tax deductions. You can deduct any expense that is incurred in connection with the running of your business, from advertising and business cards to the cost of utilities or wages paid to employees. There are many tax laws that can benefit the small-business owner. Be careful, however: Even if you are legally entitled to a tax deduction, it may not always be beneficial to claim it.

There are certain items on a tax return that can trigger a taxpayer's chances of being audited. In his book *Fight the IRS and Win! A Self-Defense Guide for Taxpayers* (TAB Books, 1988), Cliff Roberson lists ways to reduce the risk of an audit and the types of items that will be most likely to trigger further examination by the IRS. Some of these audit triggers are exactly what you might expect, such as an indication of unreported income or an incorrectly prepared tax return. However, there are legal tax deductions that, if taken, may cause you more trouble than they are worth.

If you have a room in your house that is used exclusively to carry on the activities of your home business, you are entitled to a deduction for a home office. Even though this is a perfectly legal deduction, an office-in-the-home deduction is listed as a high-risk item in Roberson's book. He says, "Although no exact figures are available on this, former IRS employees indicate that home office deductions are quite frequently subjects of IRS target programs and that it will increase the DIF score of a taxpayer." (Note: DIF stands for Discriminant Function Program, which is a secret computer-screening program that selects returns with the highest potential for a significant change in tax liability.) If the amount of the home office deduction is small compared to the tax-payer's total positive income, consideration should be given to forgoing this deduction to reduce the chances of an audit.

Roberson also notes that business returns showing total adjusted gross receipts in excess of $100,000 have a greater chance of being selected for audit. And here is another reason to choose your tax preparer carefully: The IRS has a list of problem tax preparers, and if yours is on that list, your return will at least be screened manually for audit selection. The book suggests that you select a local preparer with a good reputation, one whose clients are not normally audited. "If the preparer has multiple clients being audited by the IRS," Roberson writes, "this may be an indication that the IRS has targeted that preparer."

While it is important to use your common sense when selecting a tax professional, the book suggests four specific introductory questions that should be asked during your selection process to determine how well he or she understands tax law and procedures. They are:

1. Have you ever worked for the IRS?
2. Do you regularly handle tax cases, other than tax planning and pre-audit problems?
3. What is your experience with the IRS Collections Division?
4. Which tactic should be used in my case? Why?

Roberson also suggests that you choose someone who answers your questions with ease and with apparent technical competence and speaks in clear and understandable language. You should also look for someone who is easily accessible and prompt in returning your telephone calls.

It makes no sense to start a home business and then avoid acting like a legitimate business owner. Fulfill all your legal requirements. The results of this positive step will do more than you can imagine to help your home business grow and prosper.

For more information on finances and taxes for small and home-based businesses, consult the following books: *The New Financial Guide for the Self-Employed* by John Ellis, published by Contemporary Books; and *Steps in Meeting Your Tax Obligations*, Management Aid 1.013, published by the Small Business Administration, 1441 L Street NW, Washington, D.C. 20416.

CHAPTER EIGHTEEN

HOW TO CHOOSE THE BEST HOME BUSINESS FOR YOU

Making the decision to start your own home-based business is fairly simple. The difficult problem is deciding what kind of venture it will be. To answer this question, most new entrepreneurs seek advice from friends and relatives. The problem with this approach is that if you ask ten different people, you'll get ten different answers. Eight will give you different ideas that "can't lose," and the other two will think you're totally crazy for wanting to work at home in the first place.

Reading books, taking business courses, attending motivation lectures, and discussing ideas with business people will prepare you for managing your enterprise, but these courses do little toward helping you decide what business idea would be compatible with your goals and lifestyle. And remember, just because a business is potentially profitable does not mean that it will fit your personal needs or that you will like it.

At the outset you should know that the three most common causes of small business failure are:

1. lack of working capital
2. lack of experience
3. lack of proper planning

These are important matters, to be sure, and we have addressed them in previous chapters. But what is the fourth most common cause of business failure? It is not what most people would think. Research has found that it is *the owner's lack of interest*. One of the keys to the success of your new business, therefore, is knowing which is the best business for you to start in the first place. It is vital to determine which business interests you the most—one you'll enjoy working at—and that fits your background and experience.

A good way to help you properly decide what kind of venture is best for you is to utilize the following step-by-step procedure for personal evaluation. By following this series of simple steps, you can determine if the home business venture you're considering fits your interests and needs.

WHAT TO CONSIDER

There are dozens of attributes and characteristics that one can consider when choosing a new home business to start. However, to be practical, only fifteen need to be considered in detail. The following are the characteristics against which you will measure a business or businesses you might have in mind. Consider them carefully.

1. High Income Potential

Can the prospective business produce the amount of income you want? The first consideration you should make is *how much money you want to earn*, not what you need. If a business is generating only enough income to provide for your needs, and not your wants, you won't be satisfied. Providing only for needs can be done without personal risk by taking a job working for someone else.

After you have decided how much money you expect to make, determine if your idea can provide you with that kind of money. If the majority of your competitors don't make the kind of income you hope to make, don't assume that your operation will be that much better than those already in existence.

2. Sales Calls

Do you enjoy making sales calls on clients or the challenge of making cold sales calls? If not, don't consider a business in which you will have to be the salesperson. Many people don't know what their true feelings are with respect to sales calls. If this is true for you, take a part-time evening or weekend job where you have to do this. You will find out rather quickly if it's for you!

Often, new business owners have the mistaken idea that to get customers all that is necessary is to put an ad in the newspaper. While any advertising helps, there are many endeavors that require personal contact in order to grow. Personal-service businesses are good examples of enterprises that require a lot of personal selling. Just the opposite would be a mail-order business in which all of the customers buy from your ads or catalog.

3. Morning Person or Night Person

Do you greet the early morning with energy and enthusiasm? Or do you hate getting up early? If the latter is true, don't start a wake-up call service, for example, since you'll have to be up far earlier than your customers. This could mean being awake and coherent as early as 4 or 5 A.M.

It is very important to fit the hours of the business to your built-in body clock rather than vice versa. If you must totally change your lifestyle, the chances are very good that in time you will grow to resent and even hate what you are doing.

4. Being a Homebody

Is being home virtually all the time going to drive you crazy? If you are a very socially active person and need continual contact with other people, choosing to work at home could prove very frustrating. To retain personal contact with the outside world, you may be continually tempted to break away from your home office to visit friends and neighbors or to go shopping. Your business will undoubtedly suffer.

5. Employees

In the event that your home business will need an employee or two, do you enjoy managing people? A business that requires employee management requires a great deal more effort than one that only you and/or your spouse operate. Many people dislike managing employees. Consider your thoughts and feelings on this matter before committing to a venture that might require hiring a large number of them.

6. Weekends

Will your prospective business require that you work on weekends? Many home businesses do. Will this bother you? If you are used to doing something with family or with friends each weekend, you may resent this. There are many businesses, however, that make the majority of their money on weekends. A home-based catering service, for example, certainly would suffer if it did not operate on weekends. Are you ready to make this kind of commitment?

7. Status

What are your feelings about status in your local social group or in the business community? If status is important to you, would your new enterprise adversely affect it? If you are a prominent corporate executive, running a home-based appliance-repair service would be a social comedown. Would it bother you if friends scoffed when you decided to clean carpets or recycle trash for a living?

8. Family Working with You

Are you planning to have members of your family work with you? Is it necessary for them to help in order for your business to succeed? Do they support the idea? The time to discuss this aspect of your planning is before you make a change, not after the fact.

9. Special Training

Will you need to retrain yourself in order to run your new business? Do you want to learn a new skill? Is the cost and time involved worth the end result?

Many people feel that they can't learn new trades or ideas. If this is your belief, consider only an idea that falls within your current scope of knowledge.

10. Long Hours

Many home businesses require longer hours than you may be presently working at a regular job. Can you handle this major change in your lifestyle? Can you physically take the greater workload? Will you resent the extra hours required by a new business?

11. Future Potential

Have you examined the full potential of your business? Is the market expanding and increasing for your product or service or is it going to be flat or even lose ground? If your only concern is keeping a business at a specified level, then future potential is not important. If you plan or wish to grow and expand, potential is very important.

12. Physical Stamina

Will your new business idea require physical exertion that you will not be capable of providing on an extended basis? Do you have the strength to stamp out dozens of novelty badges and buttons if that is the business you choose? Can you carry carpet-cleaning equipment up two flights of stairs? Physical-stamina requirements are an important item to consider in any endeavor.

13. Dealing with People

Some businesses will require constant daily contact with many people, some nice and others not so nice. If you don't like dealing with people, a business that entails a lot of face-to-face selling may not be a smart proposition for you. Perhaps you should consider a venture in which you deal only with other business people rather than the general public.

14. Control Your Own Hours

One of the reasons many people start home businesses is to control their own hours, and with many types of ventures this is possible. However, with many service businesses, such as catering, your hours will be dictated by your clients. So if choosing your own hours is important, steer away from those that will not allow it.

15. Fear of Technology

Some people take to new developments in technology like a duck takes to water, while others won't even attempt to change a light bulb. If a certain type of business will require you to use a computer, laser printer, fax machine, or some other specialized equipment, you must be willing to take up the challenge to master it; your instruments of business cannot intimidate you.

HOW TO EVALUATE YOUR IDEA

Step #1. Carefully read through the fifteen attributes and characteristics listed above. If you feel that some others not mentioned here need to be considered, add them to the list.

Step #2. With no particular business in mind at this point, evaluate each of these attributes and characteristics as to their personal importance to you. Rank them on a scale of 1 to 4. If the consideration is a serious problem for you, rank it a 4; if it is a problem but you can deal with it, rank it a 3; if it is a slight concern but really not important, rank it a 2; and if it is of little or no concern to you, rank it a 1.

Record the ranking next to each attribute or characteristic in column 1 of the Evaluation Chart. These values will be used to weigh the evaluation of your specific business idea.

Add up the values you have written down and record the sum at the bottom of the column. Then multiply the sum by 10 and record the result at the bottom of the column.

Step #3. Next, evaluate your business idea. Consider the same attributes or characteristics listed at the left and evaluate how close the proposed business comes to fitting your needs or desires. This time use a ranking scale from 1 to 10. Consider 1 as the worst possible match and 10 as the best possible match to your needs and thoughts.

Record these values in column 2 of the chart.

Step #4. After you have finished rating the potential business (Step #3), multiply the values in column 1 (Step #2) times the rankings you placed in column 2 (Step #3) for each of the fifteen business attributes and characteristics. Place these values in column 3. The result will be your "weighted" value for that attribute or characteristic considered.

Now add up the total of these "weighted" values in column 3 and record the sum at the bottom of that column. (Note that columns 4 and 5 allow you to evaluate a second business for comparison.)

Step #5. Divide the weighted sum of column 3 by the weighted sum of column 1. The resulting percentage will tell you how close the business in question comes to satisfying your needs and those attributes you consider important in a business.

Obviously, 100 percent means the business is a perfect match. A 50-percent answer indicates that the business in question will be only halfway satisfying to your needs. Values below 50 percent can be considered as probably being a very bad match; a business with this low value will probably make you unhappy and perhaps fail.

The majority of successful businesses fall between a 60 and 80 percent ranking. It is very rare that a business will score a 100-percent match. Of course, a good match alone will not guarantee business success. Your undertaking still must be well planned, adequately financed, and executed with lots of good hard work.

EVALUATION CHART

Example: John and Betty were trying to decide between starting a catering business or a desktop publishing service. Both sounded like good ideas. Here's how they filled out the chart on page 131, as outlined in the preceding steps. You can fill in your own rankings in the blank form on page 132. Note that there is space in which to evaluate two different businesses.

A) Add up the values you entered in column 1 and enter the total at the bottom of the column. Now multiply that figure by 10:
$$46 \times 10 = 460$$

B) To find the weighted value of the first business (the catering business in the example), rank the 15 attributes and record their values in column 2. Then multiply the values in column 1 times the values in column 2 and record the result in column 3.

C) To calculate the "match factor" for the first business, divide the sum for column 3 by the weighted attribute total calculated in "A" above:
$$178 \div 460 = .39 \text{ or } 39\%$$

D) To calculate the "match factor" for the second business (the desktop publishing business in the example), repeat the process: Multiply the values of column 1 times the values of column 4 and enter the result in column 5. Divide the sum of column 5 by the weighted attribute total calculated in "A" above:
$$339 \div 460 = .74 \text{ or } 74\%$$

Business Attribute to Consider	Column 1 Personal Value Rating	Column 2 Business #1 Value	Column 3 Col. 1 × Col. 2	Column 4 Business #2 Value	Column 5 Col. 1 × Col. 4
1. Income potential	4	4	16	8	32
2. Sales calls	1	10	10	5	5
3. Lifestyle	4	1	4	10	40
4. Being a homebody	4	1	4	3	12
5. Employees	1	7	7	5	5
6. Weekends	4	1	4	8	32
7. Status	4	3	12	8	32
8. Family work	1	5	5	8	8
9. Special training	4	8	32	5	20
10. Long hours–	4	10	40	5	20
11. Future potential	4	2	8	8	32
12. Physical stamina	1	2	2	9	9
13. Dealing w/people	2	7	14	8	16
14. Control hours	4	3	12	9	36
15. Fear of technology	4	2	8	10	40
Totals	46		178		339

Business Attribute to Consider	Column 1 Personal Value Rating	Column 2 Business #1 Value (cater)	Column 3 Col. 1 × Col. 2	Column 4 Business #2 Value (desktop)	Column 5 Col. 1 × Col. 4
1. Income potential					
2. Sales calls					
3. Lifestyle					
4. Being a homebody					
5. Employees					
6. Weekends					
7. Status					
8. Family work					
9. Special training					
10. Long hours					
11. Future potential					
12. Physical stamina					
13. Dealing w/people					
14. Control hours					
15. Fear of technology					
Totals					

Remember that a home business idea does not have to be complicated to be successful, nor does it necessarily require a large investment. Don't overlook the most obvious choices when you are trying to
decide on a business idea. The best possibilities are the things you have
been doing all of your life for your family, or for your own pleasure.
When you choose an idea that you will enjoy, and fill your hours with
activities you love, the money you want will easily follow.

CHAPTER NINETEEN

100 HOME BUSINESS IDEAS

What kind of business can you run from your home? While some home entrepreneurs pursue the traditional occupations we associate with home work such as refinishing furniture, tutoring, and producing arts and crafts, many others have found they can use the skills they learned while working for someone else to start their own business. Generally, any type of work you have done for an employer can be used to develop your own business. Working as a salesperson, auto mechanic, writer, accountant, teacher, realtor, and computer operator are examples of experiences that can be used to start a home business. Also, mothers can build a business based on their experiences in child care, cooking, decorating, and management.

Some people operate small manufacturing businesses out of their garages or basements while others set up service-oriented businesses in their kitchens or trucks; some have discovered the lucrative field of importing goods, and others have tucked mail-order companies into spare rooms since they don't need a storefront but only a mailbox and space for inventory for this type of business.

There is a growing industry linked to the high-tech market. As high-technology becomes available and affordable, and computers become increasingly "user friendly," even more people will be attracted to the advantages of doing computer work at home. Some of the computer-oriented work is for self-owned businesses, but large companies are beginning to hire homeworkers who telecommute with the main office. This type of arrangement appeals especially to those who want to work at home but aren't adventurous enough to strike out on their own.

As you are thinking about which kind of business to operate, consider where you live, your job skills, hobbies, the equipment you own, the needs of your community, and, certainly, the work you enjoy doing.

Plan for success but don't expect overnight riches. Each business is different, and you will need to find what combination of factors yields success. During the period of development, and even after the business is underway, it will take time to make a profit.

The following list of home business ideas is broken down into two main sections: *service businesses* and *product-based businesses*, each with several subdivisions. To help get you started, we have tried to include with each business idea a source that can provide more information, training, materials, tools, manuals, or other assistance. Also bear in mind that not all of these businesses are performed exclusively in the home—a lawn service, for example. But your home will be the base of operations, where you make your plans, do your paperwork, prepare your advertising, and handle your bookkeeping.

SERVICE BUSINESSES

Consulting and Counseling

Accounting. The "simplified" tax code has the public more confused than ever. If you are an accountant for a company, you can earn excellent part-time profits by offering tax consultation and tax preparation in your community. If you're not trained as an accountant, you can receive education from various sources including: H&R Block, 1-800-7TAXLAW; National Tax Training, Monsey, NY 10952; Federated Tax Service, 2021 W. Montrose Ave., Chicago, IL 60618 (free info). For other information about this business, write to: National Association of Accountants, Small Business Advisory, 10 Tarragon Drive, PO Box 433, Montvale, NJ 17645.

Astrology. People have been fascinated by astrology for millennia, and today's interest in New Age thinking and materials makes it as popular as ever. If you have some expertise in this area, you can profit by giving astrological profiles, biorhythms, Tarot readings, and the like. You can acquire expertise by visiting your local library and reading everything you can find on the subject. Community bulletin boards may be the best way to advertise this type of business. One astrology reader on Long Island, New York, was hired by a restaurant to give readings to patrons as they waited for their meals.

Business Consulting. Consulting is probably the fastest-growing home business, and potentially one of the most profitable. If you have worked in a particular field for many years, and feel that you have some expertise that you can share with other businesses, you can demand respectable fees for that knowledge. Advertise via direct mail to potential business customers. Explain your background, what you have to offer, and, most important, how your knowledge can increase their profits or efficiency. Get more information from: *Consulting Opportunities Journal*, published by Consultants National Resource Center, 500 Kaetzel Road, Gapland, MD 21736.

Career Counseling. Older citizens who have decades of experience in the workplace can advise college graduates or those thinking of starting a business. You can help these individuals with a step-by-step approach to choosing the right vocation based on their backgrounds and interests. One helpful book might be *An Introduction to Counseling: A Handbook* by J.R. Engelkes and D. Vandergoot; published by Houghton Mifflin Co., 2 Park Street, Boston, MA 02108.

Credit Counseling. There are thousands of people who have gotten into trouble with their credit cards and need a way out. You can help by explaining the various methods of dealing with creditors, establishing and maintaining a household budget, and fixing credit records. For more information on starting this business, write to: Professional Credit Counselors, 18912 Brookhurst, Fountain Valley, CA 92708.

Computer-Based Services

Computer Consulting. As the computer pervades almost every aspect of our daily lives, people need to become computer literate—or at least know how to work the things. If you have basic computer knowledge as well as specific expertise with popular software (Word Perfect, Lotus 1-2-3, etc.), individuals and other businesses will find your help worth paying for. You can have clients come to your home, but they might feel more comfortable if you came to their homes to work on their own machines. Of course, if you consult for business, you *must* go to them.

Advertise in the Yellow Pages or send direct-mail queries to business offices that you know use computers. Check your local computer dealers and ask about businesses that have just bought computer systems—you *know* they'll need help, and the dealer usually isn't interested in helping customers work the things once they've made the sale. In fact, you might be able to make a deal with the computer dealer in which he recommends you as a consultant. For further reading: *The Computer Consultant*, Schueler Communications, Inc., 208 N. Townsend Street, Syracuse, NY 13203.

Computer Programming. No software package right out of the box is going to work for a business exactly the way they want it to, so custom computer programming is often needed. Your programming ability can create custom programs for retailers and other businesses. If this idea interests you but you don't know programming, a home-study course is available from International Correspondence Schools, 925 Oak Street, Scranton, PA 18508-9989.

Newsletter Publishing. The computer is quickly revolutionizing the publishing business. With the right software, fonts, and printers, you can have a mini-publishing business in your home. With programs such as Aldus PageMaker and Xerox Ventura Publisher for the IBM PC and Macintosh, and Professional Page and Pagestream for the Amiga, you can produce professional-quality newsletters, brochures, and other printed items for individuals and businesses. There are many books available (check your library or bookstore) that can help you successfully use the above-mentioned software. The Newsletter Association (1401 Wilson Boulevard, Suite 403, Arlington, VA 22209) publishes *Guidebook on Newsletter Publishing* and *Success in Newsletter Publishing: A Practical Guide*. Write for current prices.

Self-Publishing. You could also publish your own works. Selling how-to reports, manuals, and booklets can be a very lucrative business. You don't necessarily need a computer, but it sure makes it easier. Advertise your publications through classified ads in subject-specific periodicals. For example, if you publish a booklet on raising canaries, run the ad in magazines edited for bird owners (there are magazines for virtually every interest, and most carry classified ads). For further reading, check your library or write for: *The Complete Guide to Self-Publishing* by Tom and Marilyn Ross, from Writer's Digest Books, 9933 Alliance Road, Cincinnati, OH 45242.

Entertainment Services

Clowning. This business is no laughing matter. Decent profits can be earned from doing your funny business at children's parties and schools. Contact nursery schools, pre-kindergarten classes, and day-care centers and offer your services. The schools may not be able to pay much, so birthday parties are probably your best bet. Advertise on community bulletin boards and in local shopper papers. Two publications worth getting are: *Creative Clowning*, Java Publishing Co., 6510 Lehman Dr., Colorado Springs, CO 80918; and *Start a Clowning Business* by Donna Huff, 203 State Road, Sellersville, PA 18960.

DJ Service. Good disk jockeys are still in demand for large parties of all kinds: birthdays, anniversaries, small weddings, office parties, dances, etc. You'll need a large selection of popular dance tunes that covers a wide variety of tastes and styles, and quality sound equipment that is both portable and powerful enough to project throughout a large auditorium. You might consider staging your own dance weekends at a resort, charging per couple. Place ads in the Yellow Pages for this service.

Homeowner Services

Appliance Moving. People who are renovating their kitchens or are having new appliances installed need heavy refrigerators, stoves, ranges, dishwashers, freezers, and sinks moved. With some basic knowledge of plumbing, electronics, and gas works (for disconnection and connection purposes), a strong back, and a hand dolly, you can be in business. Be sure to advertise that you will disconnect and reinstall all appliances for your clients, and offer to clean them as well.

Closet Organization. Believe it or not, this is a booming business. Several franchises in this field have even sprung up in the past few years. But you don't need a franchise if you have a good sense of space and organization. With a knack for woodworking or the now-popular use of colorful plastic-coated wire baskets and racks, you can provide a much-needed service for thousands of homeowners in your community. This is especially needed because most houses built in the last twenty years have put a premium on space, and that usually means small closets. The plastic-coated wire racks make closet organization especially easy and provide the most flexibility with design; most home-improvement centers sell them.

Garage Sale Organizer. Sure you can make some money with your own garage sale, but you can make much more by becoming a professional. You can organize and run garage sales for dozens of households in your town. Your sales pitch is that you know what sells and what doesn't, how to price objects, how to attract customers, and what to serve (such as free coffee). As the organizer, you can either charge a flat fee for your services or accept a percentage of the total take. But you must insist that you run the show, and that your decisions on pricing and display are not questioned. Look for the book *Garage Sale Mania* by Chris H. Stevenson; Betterway Publications, Box 219, Crozet, VA 22932.

Hauling, Light. If you have a pickup, there are numerous tasks you can undertake for customers: hauling trash, dirt, appliances, lumber, etc. Advertise your services on bulletin boards and in the local Penny-Saver. Suggested reading: *How to Earn $15 to $50 an Hour and More with a Pickup Truck or Van* by Don Lilly; available from Darian Books, 4909 W. Joyce Circle, Glendale, AZ 85308.

Housesitting Service. When families stayed put, it used to be possible for some member of the family to feed the pets, water the plants, and take in the mail on those rare occasions when someone was absent from home. But in today's mobile society, a homeowner will often have no family member living in the same town and won't even know the neighbors. So the need for housesitters keeps growing. You can provide that service, either as a sitter yourself, or as a manager of a group of housesitters. For a comprehensive manual on how to start and operate this business, write for *How to Run a Housesitting Business* by Jane Poston, 1708 E. 9th Street, Tucson, AZ 85719.

Interior Decorating. If you have a flair for design, an eye for color, and good managerial skills, you too could have your own decorating business. You can charge customers for design time and for the resale of goods that you purchase for a particular project, such as decorating fabrics and mini-blinds. Serve both residential and commercial businesses and offer consulting services on lighting, window coverings, and more. Take customers to merchandise showrooms where they can see what goods you have access to. When you do business with a new supplier, fill out a credit application with them. Then set up a credit line or a cash-on-delivery account. Recommended reading: *Interior Decorator's Handbook*, Columbia Communications, 370 Lexington Avenue, New York, NY 10164.

Laundry Service. There are many services you can provide for the modern single or modern couple, both of whom work, and laundry is one of them. You'll need a large-capacity, heavy-duty washing machine and the inclination to wash, dry, and fold clothes all day. But substantial profits are there for the taking. This service might be perfect in an apartment building where the tenants must share washers and dryers. The apartment dwellers (most of whom dread doing the laundry anyway) will pay for the coin-operated machines *plus* your fee. As an added service, you can offer to take clients' suits, dresses, and coats to be dry cleaned, and deliver them when done.

Instruction and Tutoring

Aerobic Instruction. There is no end in sight to America's penchant for fitness. If your finished basement is large enough, you can hold exercise and fitness classes for men and women in your community. If you don't have the space, see about leasing it at the local YMCA, YWCA, or other such facility. Study nutrition and offer a complete package of nutrition and exercise guidance. To find out about aerobics certification, contact the Aerobics and Fitness Association, 15250 Ventura Boulevard, Suite 310, Sherman Oaks, CA 91403.

Ceramic Instruction. This craft is popular among adults as well as children. If you're experienced in creating colorful ceramics, you can give lessons from your kitchen or workroom. For some creative ideas, these publications will be helpful: *Ceramics*, Duncan Enterprises, 5661 Shields Avenue, Fresno, CA 93727. *Ceramic Projects, Ceramic Arts and Crafts*, 30595 W. Eight Mile Road, Livonia, MI 48152. National Council for Education for the Ceramic Arts, PO Box 1677, Bandon, OR 97411.

Music Instruction. Whether or not rock and roll is to thank for it, today's kids are as interested in music as ever. And they'll always need lessons in piano, guitar, clarinet, etc. Schools usually provide some basic instruction, but instrument-specific, one-on-one instruction is always necessary. Your proficiency with a particular instrument could be the basis of your home-based business. If your instrument is a popular one such as piano, you can schedule enough lessons to keep you busy practically all day every day. Advertise everywhere: school and community bulletin boards, local shopper papers, and the Yellow Pages.

Matchmaking Services

Agent/Entertainment. You can be a go-between for local talent and businesses and individuals seeking entertainers for parties. To build a roster of entertainers, begin by scouring advertisements in local newspapers and magazines, by telephoning libraries, schools, cultural centers, camps, and Y's. Place ads in local newspapers to recruit various types of entertainers. When you attend fairs, concerts, parties, and other events, evaluate the performers and pursue those that look good to you. Carry a generous supply of business cards to give to possible clients and to performers you think may be effective. (Note: All states with major entertainment industries require agents to be licensed, then franchised by the Screen Actors Guild. The best way to gain experience is with an entry-level position in an agency, or acquire a law degree.)

Apartment Rental List. With a simple home computer you can become an apartment broker finding renters for empty apartments. Allow the apartment owner to list her or his rental for free; your profits come from the renter who pays you for finding the space. Add a printer to your computer and you can publish a local paper of available rentals. On the flip side, you can also be an apartment locator. Students and other individuals looking for apartments can come to you for help. Apartment buildings and homes with rooms to let will gladly place their names with you.

Dating Service. As the number of single Americans keeps expanding in all age groups and income brackets, businesses to help them find companionship are needed. Many dating services have been started with a box of file cards and some eager clients. A home computer now makes the task easier, but is not necessary. Collect pertinent data on your clients, make matches, and set up dates. For a set fee, you provide each applicant with five names to contact. Then let nature take its course. One company that can help get you started is Selectra-Date Corporation, 2175 Lemoine Ave., Ft. Lee, NJ 07024.

Roommate Service. The growing number of unmarried Americans has led to the development of this match-up industry that is easily run from one's home. You'll find roommates for people who prefer not to live alone or can't afford to. High rents and mortgages, the soaring divorce rate, and the inability of salaries to keep pace with inflation are sending more and more singles in search of roommates. For assistance in starting this type of business, contact: Room-Mate Referral, 8139 S. I-35, Oklahoma City, OK 73149.

Personal Services

Adult Day-Care Center. Elderly citizens with no one to care for them is a growing problem in the U.S. and it's only going to get worse. With this business you can earn an income while providing a much-needed service. For more information contact: National Council of the Aging, National Institute of Adult Day Care, 600 Maryland Avenue, SW, West Wing 100, Washington, D.C. 20024. Ask about their numerous publications, including *Developing Adult Day Care*.

Answering Service. When you install an extra phone line (or several, depending on the size of your business) in your home, busy people can have their calls call-forwarded to you. You take messages for them. The only caveat with this business is that you have to be home *all* the time (or at least during the hours that you establish) to answer the phone. A manual, *Telephone Answering Service*, is available from American Entrepreneurs Association, 2311 Pontius Avenue, Los Angeles, CA 90064. A newsletter entitled *The Message* is available from the Association of Telephone Answering Services, 29 W. 57th Street, New York, NY 10019.

Babysitting. The old standby is still a moneymaker—even more so, in fact, because mothers are busier than ever. A more lucrative angle to babysitting is to become a babysitting broker. You advertise the service in various locations, then have a number of baby-sitters on call. That way, parents can always be assured of getting a sitter when they need one. As a broker, you take a percentage (10 percent) of what the sitter earns. For more information: *The Complete Babysitter's Handbook* by Elizabeth James and Carol Barkin; Julian Messner, 1230 Avenue of the Americas, New York, NY 10020.

Bed and Breakfast/Homestays. Turn your home into a welcome haven for travelers and tourists. Unlike full-fledged B & Bs, homestays usually have just one or two rooms available for paying guests. They are for young couples struggling to pay off a mortgage, or for retired couples interested in a part-time business. Homestays allow homeowners to turn extra rooms into extra dollars. Of course, not every home will make a good bed-and-breakfast homestay. Nor are all people cut out for being a B & B host/owner. A prospective host/owner should enjoy meeting all kinds of people, like to cook, enjoy entertaining visitors, keep the house clean and neat, and live in an area that is attractive to visitors. You can obtain more information from: National Bed and Breakfast Association, PO Box 332, Norwalk, CT 06853; American Bed and Breakfast Association, PO Box 23294, Washington, D.C. 20026.

Calligraphy Service. If you already know how to do calligraphy, the art of beautiful writing, there's a market for your talents among those needing special invitations, personalized greeting cards, diplomas, and certificates. You'll need calligraphy pens or markers, available from any art supply store. The business cards you have printed up should be done, of course, in calligraphy—it is at once an advertisement for your business and a demonstration of your skills. If you don't know how to do calligraphy, you can learn from the publication *Calligraphy For Fun & Profit*, available from E.A. Morgan Publishing Co., PO Box 1375, Huntington, NY 11743.

Chauffeur/Limousine Service. Everybody wants to go in style to weddings, concerts, business meetings, even funerals. And what better way to go than in a fully equipped, chauffeur-driven limousine? In the style-conscious 1990s, when image is everything, more and more people are doing it to propose marriage, celebrate an anniversary, close a business deal, or go to the theater. You as a limo provider and/or driver can cash in to the tune of $40 to $125 an hour on each car. Check with your State Department of Motor Vehicle Licensing for special license requirements.

Child Day-Care Center. Today, when more and more mothers are working outside the home, the need for quality child-care increases. Add the fact that many parents prefer a "home" setting for their child, especially the very young ones, and you can see that the market is quite large for this service. It is a service that can be operated by mothers of any age—or even a retired couple—and it doesn't take a large investment to get started. When considering a home day-care service, you will need to do some research. Home day-care providers are often regulated just as day-care centers are. Call and talk with the local agency of family and children services. They can advise you on the licensing or registration requirements you will be expected to follow. These requirements cover such things as how many children you may have in your care, how much space you need for each child, and appropriate meals and snacks. They may also offer classes in child care and development that you may want to, or be required to, attend. By registering with family and children services and following their recommendations, you can gain added credibility with your new clients. While planning a home day-care service, you should do your own survey of which day-care options are currently available in your area. These might include nonprofit centers such as churches, or privately run, for-profit day-care centers. A telephone call or visit to these centers can give you information that will enable you to set a competitive fee as well as find out whether or not they have a waiting list and what age children they take. If all the centers you talk with are full and have waiting lists, then you know many people are looking for day care. Also, if they don't provide care for certain ages—very young infants or after-school children, for example—that could be the market you should go after. Charge by the day or the week. Rates run between $150 and $200 per month per child. Be certain of insurance regulations and your personal liability. A recommended book is *So You Want to Open a Profitable Day-Care Center* by Patricia Gallagher, PO Box 555, Worcester, PA 19490.

Engraving. Customers will pay a premium price for glass, stone, and metal that is custom engraved with their names or designs of choice. The National Association of Professional Engravers (21010 Center Ridge Road, Rocky River, OH 44116) offers educational instruction, information, and certification.

Genealogy. The family tree that everyone has may be the money tree you've been looking for. Genealogical research is the third-most popular hobby in the U.S., so earn money hunting down ancestors. One personal quality helpful for success is curiosity. After the initial steps of talking to relatives, scouting out the family Bible, rummaging through salvaged birth or death certificates and wills, and locating everything possible from family sources, you have to broaden your research to the National Archives. There are offices in Washington, Boston, New York, Philadelphia, Atlanta, Chicago, Kansas City, Fort Worth, Denver, Los Angeles, San Francisco, and Seattle. And in Utah, The Church of Jesus Christ of Latter-Day Saints (The Mormons) has the largest genealogical library in the world. You might get more information from the National Genealogical Society, 4527 17th Street North, Arlington, VA 22207.

Graphology. Become an expert at graphology—handwriting analysis—and set up shop in your parlor, or perform your service at parties, flea markets, and other get-togethers. This is a service that can also be easily offered via mail. Ask about correspondence-course certification from the International Graphoanalysis Society, 111 N. Canal Street, Chicago, IL 60606. Or obtain the following books: *Handwriting Tells; What Your Handwriting Reveals*; and *Handwriting Analysis Made Easy*, each available from E.A. Morgan Publishing Co., PO Box 1375, Huntington, NY 11743.

Grocery Delivery. There aren't many grocery stores or super-markets that deliver groceries to customers anymore, but with the increasing number of two-income families and the increasing demand on leisure time, grocery delivery is once again needed. So why don't you take up the slack? Here's how you might work it: Arrange with a supermarket to buy groceries at a discount (because you're buying in quantity) and deliver them to your customers. During its first week in business, a company called Grocery Express, in Memphis, Tennessee, made seventy-six deliveries—$2,600 worth of groceries, of which they kept 10 percent.

Home Hairstylist. The elderly and otherwise homebound can always get a visiting nurse, but it's difficult to find a hairdresser who will make house calls. There's your opportunity if you have hairstyling skills. In the privacy of a hospital room or their home, your customers can get cuts, colors, shampoos, perms, maybe even manicures. If you want to think big, you can run an entire network of home hairstylists; licensed hairdressers and cosmetologists might agree to work for you on an "on-call" basis.

Party Planner. Be a professional party thrower for individuals and businesses. Find the right location, arrange for entertainment, provide the food and decorations—the whole works. For supplies, contact: Party Time, Inc., 395 94th Avenue, NW, Minneapolis, MN 55433.

Patent Searcher. Would-be inventors usually don't want to spend the time or go through the arduous task of performing a patent search. But if you have the patience and live near a patent depository library, you can provide this service for a good fee. To conduct the search you will have to go to the Patent Deposit Library in your state (most states have at least one); call or write to the Patent Trademark Office, Washington, D.C. 20231 (703-557-3341) to find the one nearest you. If you have a home computer, you can conduct the search through an on-line database; contact Patsearch, Pergamon Infoline, 1340 Old Chain Bridge Road, McLean, VA 22101.

Résumé Writing. Before anyone embarks on a job search—whether he is a veteran in the work force or a recent college graduate—he'll need a résumé. Since résumés play such an important role in a job hunt, they demand special attention. Writing, designing (choosing paper, typeface, and format), and producing them may be a job that you have a knack for doing. You may have heard about résumé-writing services, but never knew how they alone could sustain a business. This service, though, is something that is always in demand, can easily branch out into other forms of typing services. It requires little overhead and start-up capital. Two good books on the subject are: *The Résumé Catalog: 200 Damn Good Examples* by Yana Parker, Ten Speed Press, PO Box 7123, Berkeley, CA 94707; *Résumés That Work* by Tom Cowan, New American Library, 1633 Broadway, New York, NY 10019.

Videotaping Service. With your camcorder you can produce "mini-movies" of weddings, baptisms, bar mitzvahs, family picnics, and birthday parties. Other ideas include video inventory for insurance purposes and video yearbooks for high schools and colleges. You may need more than one camera (and more than one operator) and some editing equipment for professional results. One book on the subject is: *How to Make Money with Your Video Camera* by Ted Schwarz; Prentice Hall, Englewood Cliffs, NJ.

Pet-Related Services

Animal Breeding. Your love of animals can be a profitable business. Breed birds, tropical fish, pedigree dogs and cats, hamsters, gerbils—whichever animal you love. Check local zoning ordinances for conducting this type of business. For more information, write: Von Saar, 860 Calle Jon, Thousand Oaks, CA 91360. The American Kennel Club (51 Madison Avenue, New York, NY 10010) is the governing body of all purebreds, registrations, and recognized shows.

Boarding Pets. When their owners go off on vacation, dogs, cats, birds, and other pets require looking after. You'll have to have the proper facilities to care for them, of course, plus a genuine love for animals. You may get more information from: American Boarding

Kennel Association, 4575 Galley Road, Suite 400 A, Colorado Springs, CO 80915.

Dog Grooming. Pet lovers who want to keep their pooches in tiptop form will be your customers. Contact: National Dog Groomers Association of America, Box 101, Clark, PA 16113. It publishes *Groomers Voice* and has a licensing committee.

Repair and Maintenance Services

Air-Conditioning Installation. Operate your own business installing, cleaning, and repairing air conditioners for homes and offices. You'll probably need a van or pickup plus the appropriate tools. A few ways to learn how to make the repairs are through home-study courses available from: NRI Schools, McGraw-Hill Continuing Education Center, 3939 Wisconsin Avenue, Washington, D.C. 20016 (air conditioning/refrigeration course); Air Conditioning Contractors of America, 1513 16th Street, NW, Washington, D.C. 20036, Attn: Christie Higgins, Exec. Asst. (offers residential short course on a fall-to-spring schedule—$275 fee). Note: licensing is required in most states.

Apartment/House Cleaning. Start your own maid service for apartment buildings or home residences. House cleaning is one business that doesn't require special training. Most women and men have been doing it in their own homes for years. Today, even teenagers are providing single and team-cleaning services in their after-school hours and during summer vacation. Put a listing in the Yellow Pages or in the local shopper paper; put up notices on community bulletin boards. If your service is thorough and reliable, you'll acquire new customers through word of mouth. Be sure to spell out to your clients exactly what duties you will and will not perform. For more information: *How to Start Your Own Maid Service* by Faye Saxon Horton, 422 Front Avenue, West Haven, CT 06516.

Appliance/Electronics Repair. Another opportunity for those who know how to wield a screwdriver and pliers. Your workshop can be a fix-it place for toasters, microwaves, blenders, food processors, and more. Home study courses in appliance servicing and electronics are offered by NRI Schools, McGraw-Hill Continuing Education Center, 3939 Wisconsin Avenue, Washington, D.C. 20016; a course in electronics is available from International Correspondence Schools, 925 Oak Street, Scranton, PA 18508-9989.

Auto Customizing. Auto enthusiasts—especially teens—are prime customers for this service, which you can operate out of your garage. To learn more about it, take a look at: *Automotive Rebuilder*, Babcox Building, 11 S. Forge Street, Akron, OH 44304; *Autobody Supply and Equipment Market*, published by Motor and Equipment Manufacturers Association, PO Box 1638, 300 Sylvan Avenue, Englewood Cliffs, NJ 07632; *Auto Trim News*, published by National Association of Auto Trim Shops, 1623 Grand Avenue, Baldwin, NY 11510.

Auto Tune-ups. Many times, specializing in a single service can really bring in the customers. Turn your garage into a business that just performs auto tune-ups. Be careful of local zoning laws, however. If you don't have adequate space in your garage, consider a *mobile* auto fix-up service (since many cars may not be in running condition to come to you anyway). You can perform tune-ups, oil changes, tire rotation and replacement, fluid changes, and even auto cleaning all from a well-equipped van. A home study course in Automotive Servicing is available from NRI Schools, McGraw-Hill Continuing Education Center, 3939 Wisconsin Avenue, Washington, D.C. 20016.

Bathtub Repair. You can refinish porcelain sinks, bathtubs, and other fixtures for homes, hotels, and motels. For start-up information and materials, write to: Kott Koatings, 23281 Vista Grande Drive, Suite B, Laguna Hills, CA 92653.

Bicycle Repair. If you like working with your hands, don't mind getting a bit dirty, and have an interest in getting paid while you learn a mechanical skill, then the bicycle business is where you can take a ride on the road to good part-time profits. Part-time mechanics command $25 per hour for their labor. It is not uncommon for the twenty-hour-per-week bike-repair business to earn over $20,000 per year. And the great thing about it is that you can start immediately, purchase the necessary tools, and acquire the skills as you go along. Plus, because bicycle riding is becoming increasingly popular with the young and old alike, ace mechanics will be in demand far into the next century. If you are mechanically inclined or have a good working knowledge of bicycles, then you're all set. Make yourself known to the schools and bike clubs. If you need to learn how to repair bicycles, a manual and bicycle repair business system is available from: Bicycle Repair of America, PO Box 24106, Minneapolis, MN 55424.

Carpet Cleaning. This is the type of business for which a demand will never lessen. With the right kind of equipment you can "clean up," so to speak. Quality equipment is available from Von Schrader Co., 1600 Junction Avenue, Racine, WI 53403. With it you can clean carpets, walls, and furniture.

Chimney Sweep. Fireplaces and wood stoves are more popular than ever, which means there's opportunity in cleaning chimneys. In your advertising, stress that dirty fireplaces are a serious fire hazard as creosote builds up inside the chimney and can combust. For supplies, contact: Copperfield Chimney Supply, 1-800-247-3305. Or write to: National Chimney Sweep Guild, PO Box 1078, Merrimack, NH 03054.

Driveway Finisher. Many homeowners like to have their driveways resealed and recoated with blacktop every year or every other year. But it's a messy, time-consuming task. Hence, an opportunity for you. You'll need a pickup in which to carry your tools, blacktop, and sealer which you can probably get at discount if you buy in quantity. Ads in local shopper papers and the Yellow Pages probably work best.

Floor-Tile Installation. Install floor tiles and sheet linoleum for customers in your community. Charge by the square foot. Laying ceramic tile for kitchens and bathrooms and wood stripping for other rooms is more difficult, but easily learned from a number of how-to sources. Knowing both skills makes you a complete floor installer.

Furniture Refinishing/Repair. Rockers with loose spindles, tables with wobbly legs . . . they can all come into your home workshop in sad condition and leave in tiptop shape. Also, people like to buy furniture from these so-called naked furniture shops with the hopes of saving some money by finishing it themselves; often, however, they never get around to it or chicken out. Perhaps you can even affiliate yourself with a naked furniture shop that will refer customers to you as a finisher.

Handyman Service. Maintaining and beautifying a home can be an endless and expensive struggle. Walls and window trim are forever in need of paint; shrubs and bushes require yearly trimming; and light carpentry and yard work are seasonal chores that face every home-owner. Weekends, which were once reserved for home improvements, are now a time to shop for necessities or leisure activities. Many people who work forty-hour weeks are not inclined to pick up a paintbrush or seal their driveway. Usually, people hire an expensive professional to do the job. The double-income family is less burdened by professional prices, but is most likely sensitive about giving their hard-earned money away. This is especially true if there is a possibility of getting the job done for a considerably lesser amount. In addition, senior citizens often own homes that are in need of repair. The high prices of a professional can restrict a cost-conscious elderly person from having work done, especially when certain necessary home improvements are small and do not require a professional. An inexpensive odd-job service is an alternative to all these problems. There is a definite need for such a service, and an odd-jobs venture, if executed with vigor and integrity, can be the start of a very profitable business. Opportunities for household odd-jobs exist wherever there are homes and homeowners, rich or poor, who must contend with the upkeep of their property. The amount of time required to run and develop an odd-jobs company depends upon the number of customers you attract as well as the amount of time you want to invest. You need not take on jobs that require sophisticated equipment. However, as you develop capital, you might invest in a used lawnmower or electric hedge clipper. These investments will enable you to expand your services to weekly yard work.

House Painter. House painting is a chore that most homeowners need, sooner or later, but often dread. You can paint the houses yourself, but it might be more profitable to organize a group of painters to work for you. You find the clients through local advertising and hire students to do the work.

Landscaping. Commercial sites as well as residential homes are in need of this service. Seed lawns, plant trees, arrange shrubs, plants, rocks, and more for a healthy fee. Some periodicals that may be of interest include: *Landscape and Irrigation*, PO Box 156, Encino, CA 91426; *Western Landscaping News*, 1700 E. Dyer Road, Suite 250, Santa Ana, CA 92705. A related business is a lawn service in which you only cut, lime, fertilize, and water lawns for a circuit of customers. Charge them by the season or per visit.

Locksmith. In this security-conscious day and age, a good locksmith is always in demand. And today, locksmiths are usually well versed in mathematics and basic electronics because of the many new types of locks being introduced. Without a full line of equipment required to handle a wide variety of jobs, you will be limiting your total income potential. The more you invest in quality equipment, the more different kinds of jobs you can handle. Equipment and a locksmithing course are available from Foley-Belsaw Locksmiths, 6301 Equitable

Road, Kansas City, MO 64120. One report worth looking at is: *How to Start Your Own Mobile Locksmithing Service* from E.A. Morgan Publishing Co., PO Box 1375, Huntington, NY 11743.

Sharpening Service. Sharpen scissors, knives, and shears for people in your community. You can get quality equipment from Serr-Edge Machine Company, 4471 W. 160th Street, Cleveland, OH 44135. If it's saw blades you're interested in sharpening, contact Foley-Belsaw Sharpening, 6301 Equitable Road, Kansas City, MO 64120.

Small Engine Repair. Fix small engines for lawnmowers, leaf blowers, chain saws, go-carts—anything that utilizes a small gasoline engine. If you have any knowledge about small gas engines (or are willing to learn) you could turn that interest into extra income. The secret is to find small gas engines, buy them cheap, and resell them at a profit. Where can you find these for five dollars or less? Check out the local flea market or ask trash haulers to set aside lawnmowers, edgers, anything with a small gas engine for you. Pay them up to $5 a shot, depending on the condition of the items. You can learn more about small gas engine repair from Foley-Belsaw Institute, 6301 Equitable Road, Kansas City, MO 64120.

Telephone Installation/Servicing. When Bob Jones needed a telephone extension put in his home, he called the phone company and was told that he'd have to wait about thirty days to be serviced. Jones did not want to wait a month just to get an extension, so he decided he would do the job himself—and his home business was born. You can operate a similar business. A working knowledge of phones, electronics, and how to run wires through walls, etc., is required. A home study course in telephone servicing is available from NRI Schools, McGraw-Hill Continuing Education Center, 3939 Wisconsin Avenue, Washington, D.C. 20016.

Upholstery Repair. Rather than buy new sofas, chairs, love seats, couches, and ottomans, people would prefer to have someone like you reupholster them. The number of people practicing this skill seems to be dwindling, so here's a real opportunity. As a part of your services, consider the making of slipcovers for the furniture. For upholstery training and tools, contact Foley-Belsaw Institute of Upholstery, 6301 Equitable Road, Kansas City, MO 64120.

VCR Repair. Just about every home that has a television now has at least one VCR that needs periodic cleaning and repair. Your garage or basement could serve as your home-based workshop. A home study course in this field is available from International Correspondence Schools, 925 Oak Street, Scranton, PA 18508-9989.

Welding/Soldering. Your garage can be the site of your soldering/ welding shop. Appeal to mechanics, stove shops, contractors, builders, and auto body shops in your area. For training, contact your State Department of Education, Adult Vocational Training Division.

Services for Other Businesses

Advertising Copywriter. If you are clever with words and have a good sense of salesmanship, there are many small businesses in your community that can use your services. You can write newspaper ads, brochures, radio ads, catalogs, and more. For more ideas, look for a copy of the *1990 Writer's Market*, Writers Digest Books, F & W Publications, 1507 Dana Avenue, Cincinnati, OH 45207.

Bookkeeping Service. This service is always in demand by businesses of all kinds. Today, you might have to have some computer experience, as many businesses are switching to computer-based bookkeeping systems. You can learn how to become a bookkeeper from these sources: National Career Institute, 2021 W. Montrose Avenue, Chicago, IL 60618; NRI Schools, McGraw-Hill Continuing Education Center, 3939 Wisconsin Avenue, Washington, D.C. 20016.

Business Secretarial Service. Take a look in your local newspaper's want ads and you'll see that good secretaries are needed. If you're quick and efficient on the keyboard, are familiar with various word processors, can take dictation or work from a dictation machine, many businesses will use your services. For more information: *Word Processing Profits at Home*, by Peggy Glenn, published by Ames-Allen Publishing, 1106 Main Street, Huntington Beach, CA 92648.

Courier Service. Deliver messages and packages for various businesses within your town. If you have a car, you can even offer to deliver parcels to neighboring towns and cities.

Office Plant-Maintenance Service. Provide and care for plants for business offices, doctors' waiting rooms, etc. For more information about such a business, contact Nancy Martelli, 1801 Lincoln Boulevard, Suite 266, Venice, CA 90291.

Research. Writers, lawyers, and publishers all need people to do research work. Most of these businesses do not have the time to put their full-time employees on necessary but time-consuming research projects. This business entails library work, phone calls, fact verification, and more, but the only ability you need is to quickly and accurately find material and enjoy digging out details. It can be quite satisfying while being educational. Offer your services via direct mail to local manufacturers, fund-raising organizations, and advertising agencies—generally any type of business that seeks specialized customers.

Typing/Word-Processing Service. Students, businesses, legal professionals, writers, and many others need reports, papers, documents, and manuscripts professionally typed. Of course it's much easier to provide this service if you have a word processor; small changes and even large rewrites can be done easily without having to retype the entire document. Post ads on school bulletin boards and send direct-mail flyers to doctors, lawyers, and any other business you can think of. One book is *How to Start and Run Your Own Word Processing Business* by Gary S. Belkin, John Wiley & Sons, 605 Third Avenue, New York, NY 10158.

PRODUCT-BASED BUSINESSES

Crafts and Hobbies

Bait Shop. Do you live near a well-stocked lake, river, bay, or stream? Fishermen will need bait, lures, line, and other equipment. You don't have to offer all of that, of course. Just posting a sign telling fishermen you have good bait worms will bring in nice profits.

Birdhouses and Supplies. Your workshop can become a birdhouse factory. Books and woodworking publications can supply designs (or design your own). You provide the labor and the selling. As a sideline you may also want to sell birdseed and other supplies. Quality birdhouses can be sold at flea markets, in specialty consignment shops, and via mail order. Contact your local home-improvement stores and hardware stores and ask if they'll sell your birdhouses on consignment.

Bronzing Keepsakes. What mother wouldn't want a bronzed remembrance of her child's babyhood? Bronzed baby shoes have long been a cherished memento adorning mantelpieces and curio shelves. You can find customers by checking registration lists at day-care centers and pre-school; these kids have outgrown their first pair of shoes, which are ready for bronzing. You can obtain materials and instructions from these companies: Nicholas Bronze Supply, 10555 U.S. Highway 98, Dept. W488, Sebring, FL 33870; or United Bronze, Rumford, RI 02916.

Cabinetmaking. For the skilled wood craftsman, making custom cabinets for kitchens and bathrooms can fetch a very high price. Use quality wood; people can get the inexpensive stuff in stores at a cheap price. So you'll be catering to an upscale clientele and should advertise where they are likely to read your ad. Expand to include other types of cabinetry and furniture making. Check your library and bookstores for design ideas. Eventually you'll be able to create a book—a catalog of sorts—of the different types of cabinets you can create.

Costume Making. Schools and local theater groups will be your prime customers year-round for this service. Of course when Halloween rolls around, you'll be sitting at your sewing machine day and night—and watching the profits roll in. Most often, people will want custom-designed costumes, but for popular costumes—witch, devil, etc.—you should check for available patterns. For theater groups that need period costumes, you will probably have to do a bit of research to be sure you have the style, materials, and colors correct.

Crafts. It's difficult to make a lot of money with most crafts unless you produce unique items quickly and inexpensively. The more unique your particular handicraft is, the more likely you will find customers for it. Most towns have antique stores or specialty gift stores that will take your crafts on consignment, provided they are convinced they will sell. An alternative to a consignment arrangement with these shops is for you to rent shelf space in the shop; then you get to keep all of the profits from your crafts sales. Flea markets are yet another outlet for well-made crafts. Still another idea is to stage home parties at which you can sell your crafts as well as those of your friends. Create a catalog of the craft items and bring some samples. You will not be selling directly at these parties, but only taking orders for items in the catalog. Naturally, the Christmas holidays will be your busiest time of the year. For sales outlets, get a copy of: *The Crafts Fair Guide* (Western), Box 5062, Mill Valley, CA 94941; Goodfellow, PO Box 4520, Berkeley, CA 94704. A good source book is *Crafts Marketing Success Secrets* by Barbara Brabec, PO Box 2137, Naperville, IL 60567.

Drapery Making/Installation. With your sewing skills, you can make custom-fitting drapes for your customers. Help them pick out the fabric and colors—you may even want to accompany your client to a fabric store to make the selection—take your measurements, then make the drapes. For an additional charge, you can hang the drapes for the customer—a chore she or he often dreads.

Dressmaking. Here's another opportunity for a good sewer. There are literally thousands of patterns from which you can help your customers choose (Vogue, Butterick, etc.). Take careful measurements and be even more careful about the quality of your workmanship. You may be especially busy around prom time. Also, heavy women or very short women who may find it difficult to find properly fitting sizes in the stores will be very grateful for your services. Advertise directly to these women in your local shopper paper ads and community bulletin boards.

Firewood Sales/Delivery. Provide seasoned firewood by the cord or by the fraction of the cord to a growing number of buyers. One angle is to buy cords of seasoned wood, then cut it into fireplace-size logs and sell fractions of the cord to a route of clients. Tell them you can bring a fresh supply of firewood every week (or however long the wood happens to last) for a set price. You can charge for each delivery or offer a special deal to provide the wood for the whole winter season.

Frame Making. Make frames of all kinds for customers' paintings, reprints, and posters. Stock a wide variety of wood and metal frames in your garage or finished basement. You will need framing skills and tools, as well as glass-cutting skills. For added profits, you can sell posters and prints of various kinds. One recommended book is: *How to Do Your Own Professional Picture Framing*, available from Tab Books, PO Box 40, Blue Ridge Summit, PA 17214.

Gift Baskets. This is one of the hottest product-oriented home businesses around. You don't have to make the wicker baskets yourself (check your Yellow Pages for a supplier), but it is up to your taste and imagination to fill them with tempting goodies. Create baskets for all occasions—birthdays, anniversaries, retirements, births, Mother's and Father's Day, Valentine's Day—or no occasion at all: an "I Miss You" gift basket. Find suppliers who will sell you the items in quantity for the best price. Put a variety of food items in the baskets along with small gifts appropriate to the occasion: satin hearts for Valentine's Day; a rattle, baby powder, and tiny undershirts for a baby's birth (gift baskets don't always have to contain food); champagne for anniversaries; etc. Decorate the baskets with ribbons and bows; the key is to make them as colorful, festive, and attractive as possible. Create a simple brochure that explains the content of each type of basket you offer, and leave them everywhere!

Glass Etching. You can etch monograms, figures, and other decorations on mugs, glasses, and plate glass. Sell them at fairs and flea markets and in consignment shops. Custom work will bring you your best prices. Quality EtchMaster equipment and instruction are available from Meistergram, 3517 W. Wendover Avenue, Greensboro, NC 27407.

House, Pet, People Portraits. Artists always seem to be struggling to get their work seen and to make a living. Here are a few ways they can do both: paint portraits of people, their pets, and their houses. People will want their portraits—or portraits of their spouses—painted as birthday or anniversary gifts. You can usually work from a good photograph if the subject is to be surprised by the painting. Pet portraits are a fast-growing service. Paint the pets in a warm and loving way— the way the owners will always want to remember them. House portraits are another service that is in demand by new homeowners and especially by realty firms that want either a sketch or full portrait done of a house for selling purposes; a painting is much more flattering and idealized than a photograph.

Monogramming. Monogram sweaters, sportswear, shirts, uniforms—you name it—with initials, logos, or designs specified by your customers. You can obtain quality equipment and a variety of lettering styles and designs from Meistergram, 3517 W. Wendover Avenue, Greensboro, NC 27407. (In Canada, call 1-800-338-8800.)

PVC Pipe Furniture. PVC stands for polyvinyl chloride, and it is now widely used in piping of all kinds. It is usually white and can be found in virtually any home improvement center, plumbing supply store, or lumberyard. This piping is so easy to work with—it is easily cut with a hacksaw—that it has become a popular framing material for making outdoor furniture. You can design and make patio chairs, chaise lounges, even porch swings with PVC pipe. The only thing you'll have to add is webbing or other material for the actual seating. Bring samples to flea markets and take orders from customers.

Stained Glass. Customers will pay a premium for well-executed stained glass. Many local stained-glass shops offer lessons, and once you become proficient at it, you can create stained-glass ornaments, gifts, even windows. A three-year program is sponsored by the Stained Glass Association of America, 8821 Bridgeport Way SW, Tacoma, WA 98499, Attention Chairman, Education Department.

Toy Design. Design and create wooden toys of all kinds for sale at flea markets, consignment shops, and home parties. Several good books are available from these two publishers: Tab Books, PO Box 40, Blue Ridge Summit, PA 17214; and Stirling Publishing Co., 2 Park Avenue, New York, NY 10016. Write for their catalogs.

Flea-Market Stand

Flea markets have come a long way since the days when they consisted of low-quality merchandise spread over rough wooden tables set up in vacant lots. That kind of flea market still exists, of course, but today's flea markets may have up to 500 booths in an air-conditioned building or several hundred booths in specially designed buildings sprawled over several acres.

Most vendors are part-timers who work flea markets two or three days a week to supplement their incomes. Others are full-timers who are trying to make a living from their efforts. Some sell fishing tackle, others sell clothing (usually imperfects), or any number of other items. Vendors range from homemakers cleaning out the garage, attic, and basement to serious business people earning a living from their stalls and stores. In between are craftspeople who are selling their own handiwork, retirees keeping busy while they supplement their incomes, and even corporations that find flea markets additional outlets for their goods.

Flea markets offer significant advantages to beginners because capital requirements are low and customer traffic—essential to a retailer—already exists. In addition, since most markets operate only two or three days a week, it is easy to start a business part-time while paying the bills through other employment.

The vendor, the market, and the merchandise: All are important. The people who fail are those who come in for four hours with a hundred dollars' worth of stock and expect to have a thousand-dollar day. In flea markets, as in any other business, you have to work for success. Successful vendors operate like a business, with regular hours and good customer service. People go to flea markets looking for bargains. That means merchandise has to be priced below other retail outlets. Look for merchandise in the directories of manufacturers available at the public library, then try the Yellow Pages as well as various state and local Chamber of Commerce publications. Other sources can be located through a variety of publications serving the field, such as *American Flea Market Journal*, a quarterly publication from M.H. Sparks, 1911 Avenue D, Brownwood, TX 76801; *The USA Flea Market Directory* from Forum Publishing Co., 383 E. Main Street, Centerport, NY 11721.

If you don't know what to sell at a flea market, here are just two ideas:

Advertising Specialties. Individuals, small businesses, and organizations are always looking for products on which to imprint their names and logos. You can provide them with these advertising specialties. For a start in this business, contact Specialty Merchandise Corp., 9401 De Soto Avenue, Chatsworth, CA 91311-4991. For further information, contact Specialty Advertising Association International, 1404 Walnut Hill Lane, Irving, TX 75038. (Publishes *Specialty Advertising Business*.)

Badge and Button Making. This is a great flea market product, or you can make custom buttons for schools, clubs, and other organizations. The buttons feature clever sayings, photos of celebrities, or, if you have a Polaroid camera, photos of your customers. You can obtain equipment from: Badge-A-Minit, 348 N. 30th Road, Box 800, LaSalle, IL 61301; Mr. Button, Box 68355, Indianapolis, IN 46268.

Food and Catering Services

Cake Sculpting/Decorating. Kitchen wizards can create specialty cakes for all occasions including birthdays, weddings, and anniversaries. Create a picture catalog to show potential customers what you're capable of making.

Catering. Quality catering is more in demand than ever before. Your culinary skill can bring in lots of profits. Home study courses are available from International Correspondence Schools, School of Catering, Oak and Pawnee streets, Scranton, PA 18518; and NRI Schools, McGraw-Hill Continuing Education Center, 3939 Wisconsin Avenue, Washington, D.C. 20016. Report: *How to Start Your Own Party Cater-*

ing Service, available from E.A. Morgan Publishing Co., PO Box 1375, Huntington, NY 11743.

Fruit and Vegetable Stand. Do you have acreage on which you can grow tomatoes, watermelon, corn, berries, and other fruits and vegetables? If so, you'll have carloads of people stopping by your roadside stand for your fresh produce. For zoning information contact your state university co-operative extension or county agent.

Herb Growing. The renewed interest in natural and organically grown foods has brought with it an interest in natural herbs. Even if you have only a small garden space in your backyard, you can grow enough herbs to support a small business. Sell the herbs to natural-food stores or start your own mail-order business selling to customers around the country via catalogs and ads in appropriate magazines.

Local Cookbook. Gather the best recipes from the best cooks in your community and publish them in a local cookbook. Have sections for appetizers, main dishes, and, of course, desserts. The contributors to the book will probably not expect any reimbursement; their name proudly attached to the recipe will be payment enough. You can find these contributors by advertising in a local paper or by contacting a local women's organization or church organization. Sell the book to area bookstores, which will often be pleased to have a book featuring local cooking talent.

Lunch Delivery. Make specialty and conventional sandwiches for delivery to hungry office workers. Create a menu of what you're prepared to offer for lunches and distribute them to every office possible in your area—you'll be surprised at the great number of orders you'll get, so be prepared. You may even need help making the lunches. If you don't want to make the lunches yourself, another angle is to arrange deals with area restaurants and delis to provide the food—you will deliver it fresh and hot. Your menu will consist of these restaurants' various house specialties. The restaurants, because you're buying in quantity, will give you a discount on the food; you mark it up further for your profit.

Mail Order

Mail order is an ideal way for you to start a home business. Basically, it's retail selling by mail. Many successful dealers have started part-time, then switched to full-time when their business began paying off.

Profits from a mail-order business can produce incomes as high as $60,000. Part-timers often take away from $5,000 to $10,000 a year if they have a good product and are willing to work hard.

A man in the Midwest invested $1,200 in promoting a stamp dispenser. His first ad, placed in the mail-order section of a big New York newspaper, brought in $3,500 in sales—amazing results that put him in a profitable business almost overnight.

A bookseller in Kansas sold over 100 million books by mail and made a fortune in the process. His product was a small, inexpensive series of books. As a means of selling them, he used ads in national magazines and mailings to his customer list.

Two persons placed an ad for printing personalized stationery in a large-circulation newspaper and were swamped with orders—$30,000 worth. Their mail-order operation got off to a tremendous start. They offered personalized stationery at a bargain price.

Mail-order success can happen instantly, but most often it requires hard work and persistence. Mail order is big business, but there is plenty of room for the small dealer. Here are some important pointers to save time, money, and false starts when you go into the mail-order business.

Pick the Right Product. The most important single factor in any successful mail-order business is the product. Pick a product or service that has been successfully sold by mail before, and one you are enthusiastic about. After you are experienced in the business, you should try unusual and different products, but in the beginning sell established ones. *Merchandise, information,* and *services* are the big three products of mail order, and they should have these qualities:

Uniqueness. Unique or exclusive products are hard to find, but examples are things you make or products that are patented or copyrighted, such as games, books, or auto accessories. When you have a good product, people will copy it, so protection is important. The stamp dispenser is a good example. You can find all kinds of variations of it available today. Another example of an exclusive or unusual service is a man in Alabama who buys and sells used correspondence courses by mail and makes good money at it.

Repeat-Sales Potential. Your customers should come back for more of the same or similar products. A good example is food—cheese, jam, and fruits. A West Coast orchard was expanded into a million-dollar business through mail-order sales of pears. Items that are consumed and need replacement meet this requirement nicely. Printing and advertising also fall into this group. A well-known clothing company began with mail sales of black raincoats to funeral directors. Good repeat-sales potential existed here, too.

High Markup Ratio. The ratio should be at least three to one. For example, you buy a product for a dollar and sell it for three. Products with a $3 to $20 selling price are best for mail order. Ideally, this means ones that are cheap to make and have a relatively high selling price. Imported items also fit this mold. Foreign labor is cheaper than American labor, and as a result your markup is often better. Books and pamphlets fall into this category, too.

Shippability. Your product should be easy to pack and ship, not breakable, and inexpensive to ship. A book, again, is a good example; it has a special low mail rate, too. You can expect to have some of your sales returned, so be sure that none are returned because of breakage.

Understandability. Make sure the product is readily understood by anyone. If you are handling auto accessories, a photograph might be used to illustrate their use.

Keep in mind that items you can personalize are very good mail-order sellers. For example: monogrammed shirts, jewelry, and stationery. Possibly the best example of a mail-order product is a book or correspondence course. It fits most of the characteristics of an ideal mail-order item.

Know How to Run Your Business. Next to the right product or service, good business sense is most important. Operating a mail-order business requires that you reach potential customers quickly and easily. This is done in three ways:

Classified Advertising. In magazines and newspapers it is used to get inquiries for your product and then follow up with your sales material. A good classified ad has several important parts. First, it attracts attention through a word or phrase. Second, it is specific. A headline for a classified ad meeting these requirements is HOW TO START YOUR OWN MAIL-ORDER BUSINESS. It rouses interest, attracts attention, and is specific. Keep it brief. Classified ads are almost always sold by the word, so you can save money by keeping it short. Write as if you were making up a telegram, and remember, at $5 a word or more, extra words are expensive! Start your ad with a good opener. In addition to the above example, here are some good, eye-catching words to use to attract attention: free, guaranteed, how to, exciting, send no money, free trial, amazing, announcing, bargain, bonus, tested, secret, you, your, new. As a complete example, here is a short but effective ad that pulls well:

HOW TO START YOUR OWN IMPORTING BUSINESS. DETAILS FREE. YOUR NAME, DEPT. A1, YOUR ADDRESS.

This ad has all the basics of a good classified ad. It's a good headline and has people appeal. It offers free information, and it's properly keyed. The key—in this case Dept. A1—provides you with a means of tracing the result of each ad; it indicates both magazine and issue. A is for the magazine, say *Income Opportunities*®, and 1 is for the issue, January 1990. This ad is specific and it gets action with the details-free offer. Asking for postage or a small amount of money cuts returns drastically, but it eliminates curiosity seekers. However, you should not try to eliminate curiosity seekers, but rather turn them into buyers. The extra effort is worth it. This is the best way for a small operator to spend his or her advertising money, and it's an easy way to get started.

Many successful dealers work only through classified ads because they have tremendous pulling power. A good ad will pull sales of three to five times the money spent on advertising, and it's an easy way to get started. For example, a $20 ad often brings back $60 to $100 in sales, and occasionally the result is phenomenal.

Display Ads. In a display ad placed in magazines and newspapers, you usually ask for the sale directly. A display ad has the same elements as a classified ad, but it also does the whole selling job. Display ads contain a headline, text explaining your product and weaving in a sales story, and a photograph or illustration of your product. They also include another staple of the mail-order business: the reply coupon. This makes response to the ad easy.

If you are not skilled in preparing ads, go to an advertising agency for help—but get one with mail-order experience! Good display ads have considerable staying power, but they are costly. No doubt you have noticed the display ads used by the bodybuilding schools; they are repeated many times without change. One famous display ad used by a music school ran for years.

When you get into mail order, become ad-conscious. Observe ad construction and when you see one repeatedly, you know it is a good one, so inspect it carefully. Display ads are used for getting inquiries too, but mostly on big-ticket items where the whole sales story can't be given in the ad.

Direct Mail. Buy or rent a mailing list and mail out your sales literature to the people on it. Select a list containing names of persons who are interested in your product. Do not use resident lists or telephone-book lists. Get a list of known buyers of mail-order items similar to your offering. List brokers and mail-order houses sell or rent lists at reasonable rates. Your best list is always your own customer list. You can't wear it out. It gives you an excellent basis for mailing new offers.

Keeping records of the results of your advertising and sales is very important. You must know the result of each ad in each magazine. When one doesn't pay off, you want to know that right away. When an inquiry is received, mark it down by day, month, year, and magazine. Answer it the same day as received. Set up a sound record-keeping system; it's necessary for improving your business and for tax records. Costs can be high in mail order, and good records will help you keep them in line. Be cost conscious. Evaluate the result of each ad monthly. Drop ads that don't pay off and replace them with ones that are substantially changed. When you change an ad, make a big change, something that can be measured. Remember, tests show one ad can outpull another by as much as twenty-five to one.

Making Sales by Mail. People appeal is the thing. Remember that your advertising and direct-mail pieces are your sales call and must offer what people want. People want to:

- *Be* in style, popular, comfortable
- *Save* money, time
- *Keep* health, possessions
- *Avoid* effort, pain
- *Achieve* comfort, pleasure, security
- *Make* profit, money
- *Attract* the opposite sex

So set up your sales material to appeal to these basic desires.

The biggest appeal in mail order is the word *free*. Give a booklet or small gift to those who inquire. Follow up with your basic offer. Offer a premium with your basic offer. For example, give a gift with each order returned within ten days. Look at the premiums offered by book clubs and record clubs. They can make money only with repeat sales, but their premium and leaders obtain customers who will provide repeat buys. People buy by mail to get bargains or things not readily available at the corner store. Be sure to include people appeal in your sales literature; it pays.

Profits and Pitfalls. Making profit in mail order can be difficult, but is definitely possible. In mail order you should do as much of the work yourself as possible. Don't hire high-priced consultants when you can get the same information from books and courses. Some packaged offers are excellent. If you must buy a package deal, mix it with your own product or service. For example, pre-printed circulars for gifts can be sent along with your own gift flyer. When you must use a package deal, try to blend it with an offer of your own. The package deal can serve to broaden your sales base, but don't use it as your whole line.

When you don't make the product yourself, set up a "drop-ship" arrangement with the manufacturer until you have proven the product and your sales package. In other words, arrange with the maker and send it to your customer when you make a sale. Later, you may want to stock an item to speed up service, give yourself more control, and reduce cost. Remember, the manufacturer will often charge you more for drop shipping, so use it sparingly.

You can find products by visiting gift shows, reading the new-products columns of magazines, visiting or calling local manufacturers, and designing items yourself. You can resurrect old items, too. Buy one of those old Sears or Ward catalogs and you may find an old product that you can turn into a modern seller. Avoid one-shot novelty items. Develop a line so repeat sales are possible. This is a basic building block of most successful mail-order businesses.

A complete start-up manual called *How to Start Your Own Mail Order Business* by the Editors of *Income Opportunities*® is available from Davis Publications, 380 Lexington Avenue, New York, NY 10017.

Party-Plan Sales

The home-party plan is a method of product marketing in which you ask a hostess or host family to sponsor a party for their friends. At this informal party you demonstrate your products. The party often includes games, refreshments (a meal, perhaps, if you demonstrate cookware), and party gifts; these variations depend on which company you choose to sell for. According to the Direct Selling Association, products often sold in this manner include clothing, cookware and flatware, cosmetics and personal-care items, decorative craft items, food supplements, household cleaning supplies, jewelry, personal products, and toys.

Each company specifies the way it prefers you stage its parties. Most party plans ask the guests to write out their orders before they leave. Some require immediate payment. Your job is to deliver the products to the individuals after the party, if it is not a cash-and-carry party. You probably should have a car at your disposal, but you might be able to get by with public transportation. It is also possible to make a deal with a friend in which both of you are dealers: The one who likes meeting people does the selling, and the one who has the car makes the deliveries.

You can move up in the ranks of your company by becoming a district manager, but you must prove an ability to sell and have the skills to motivate other salespeople. You will often work with a manager until you reach manager status, and part of your receipts, besides the average of 40-percent commission, includes gifts that range from jewelry to cars, or even trips for top salespeople. There is usually minimal paperwork involved, but many home-party representatives (often called "consultants") are expected to maintain their own inventory.

The home-party plan is a good way for the inexperienced person to learn how to sell, how to approach people, and still make money. The experienced salesperson would enjoy even more success. There is often no quota, seldom a territory, but training sessions encourage you to get out and sell more.

Pros and Cons. The advantages of the home-party plan are that you demonstrate the products in the home or office of the person who will be buying, and you show the product to more than one prospective buyer at a time. You are essentially working for yourself, but you have a company's marketing and research behind you, as well as a proven product that often has appeal to the impulse buyer. This plan is also an advantage to men and women whose work lives must be sporadic because of their home lives. If you must follow your spouse's job, as is for example often the case with military families, the home-party method of selling will enable you to keep a job and meet new people wherever you go.

A possible disadvantage would be having a manager who wants you to work more than the one day a week you originally decided upon. Another drawback, possibly, is the timing of most parties. They are often held at night, when you might be accustomed to having your family time. Certainly, you can be home during the day with your children while handling necessary phone work, but you will need a sitter for the rallies and the parties.

Best Selling Method. About 80 percent of the home-party sales force are women. This is primarily because the representatives ask women to invite them into their homes, and because the products appeal to women as both buyers and sellers. Some companies, such as those that sell cookware, appeal as well to men as representatives. One of the most successful Mary Kay cosmetics consultants is a man. Tradition is not necessarily limiting.

Years ago, when women stayed home, they had Tupperware parties and Stanley parties. This was a great form of entertainment, a way to get friends together, and a way to make money or buy a product at the same time. Today, with most women working, representatives of these companies have to be more inventive. They go where the people are. Church members have "home" parties to help stock their church nursery with toys or their fellowship kitchen with supplies. They stage bridal showers in which the bride picks out gifts and the guests pay for them as their shower gift; they also order items for themselves. Home-party representatives also hold parties in office-break rooms during lunch hours.

The tried-and-true method is to gather your best friends and their friends in the hostess's home, serve refreshments, and have a party where you demonstrate various products. If you still live in the community where you grew up, or if you know a lot of people in your town, you will have lots of contacts among friends and relatives who are just waiting for someone to become a dealer for their favorite home-party product. Once you get started, your host company may expect you to ask your hostesses and guests to become dealers also. In this way you can move up the managerial ranks, make more money, receive more prizes, and get a cut of your dealers' profits.

Many of the companies that rely on home parties do not advertise. They rely on word of mouth. You may prefer a company that supports you by advertising.

Research Before You Join. Before you decide to become a rep for a company, find out more about it by talking to your friends. Here are some questions you should find the answers to:

- What are your friends' experiences with this company?
- What is their advice?
- Is there anyone else in your community who sells for this company (in other words, is there currently competition)? Your friends may know a local dealer who would take you on as a trainee.
- Are your friends excited about this company—enough to give parties for you?
- Do the local managers press you to hold more parties than you really want to? (There is seldom a limit if you want to hold more and more parties.)
- Is the commission enough to suit you (often around 40 percent, but the amount sometimes varies by type of product or by sale price)?
- Do you want to do the paperwork if the commission schedule is complicated?
- Could you eventually afford to go full-time with this company (that is, does it sell as well as you hoped)?
- How are you paid?
- How far do you have to go to pick up your products or are they sent to you?
- Does the profit come from resales or from a large initial cost for the customer?

- Is there a charge for the starter kit (almost always there is a charge ranging from $10 to $500), or are you considered the owner of the starter kit after you have held a certain number of profitable parties?

If your friends are unfamiliar with a company, ask the local manager these questions.

Pick a company whose product you value. If you feel good about a certain product, that is a fair sign that you will be successful (as long as you don't spend all your profits). If you can't be a regular customer of this company, your lack of enthusiasm will show with prospective customers.

Consider All the Options. Another consideration is whether selling this product fits in with your lifestyle. You will probably want to be a party-plan representative while working your regular job, and work your way up to full-time manager. Contact a few companies and check the fit between their product and your lifestyle, between their local manager and your personality. You don't want to select a company, then decide that you're tired of going to rallies or of having to do back orders of products that never seem available—or that you really don't like the product. Ask questions.

If you are resourceful, using all your contacts as potential customers, you will find that many of these products will sell themselves. They are often well known or are so popular that your customers will want them immediately.

The following companies are among several that sell by the home-party plan. They use part-time contract salespeople. Although the party plans are similar, there are differences in style, payment, and commission. Thoroughly investigate each company you consider. Contact each and ask for the name and phone number of the local manager and some literature on how to get started with their business.

Mary Kay Cosmetics, 8787 Stemmons Freeway, Dallas, TX 75247; cosmetics, skin care products.

Passport Boutique, PO Box 23149, Minneapolis, MN 55423; jewelry.

Discovery Toys, 2530 Arnold Drive, Suite 400, Martinez, CA

94553; developmental toys, books, games, and tapes—most under $12.

Perfume Originals, 582A Middle Neck Road, Great Neck, NY 11023; fragrances.

The Creative Circle, 15711 South Broadway, Gardena, CA 90248; sewing crafts.

The Pampered Chef, PO Box 172, River Forest, IL 60305; kitchenware.

Watkins, Inc., 150 Liberty Street, Winona, MN 55987; household products.

For a more complete list of direct selling and party-plan selling companies, write to The Direct Selling Association, 1776 K Street NW, Suite 600, Washington, D.C. 20006; (202) 293-5760.

Index

Italics indicate a possible home business.